Praise for the *Uml*

"Well-organized, interesting and informative, Bill London's Umbrella Guide to the Inland Empire is a gem of a travel guide. Road conditions, available services, historical facts, restaurant suggestions, and other information usually available only from local residents are all included in the thirteen tours — and numerous side trips — described in detail in this valuable book."

Colleen Daly, Editor, *Oh! Idaho* magazine

"A wonderful guide and valuable resource for travelers who want to get off the beaten paths. This guide is factual, concise, and offers a myriad of choices for touring the Inland Empire."

Joan Pasco, Executive Director
Lewiston Chamber of Commerce

"Bill London's guide to one of the nation's most fascinating (but almost unpublicized) regions is a valuable addition to the library of anyone interested in this part of the country. His literate, conversational style is a pleasure to read, and his obvious feeling for the history and people of the area gives the book life."

Ed Mitchell, Publisher, *Idaho Outdoor Digest*

"I thought I knew a lot about the Inland Empire until I read Bill London's guide! This book will be as valuable to local residents as it is to visitors since it is much more than a travel guide. Interspersed within the suggested tours and sidetrips are vignettes of colorful residents, off the beaten path attractions, and non-publicized local finds."

Robert Rene, Travel Specialist
Idaho Department of Commerce

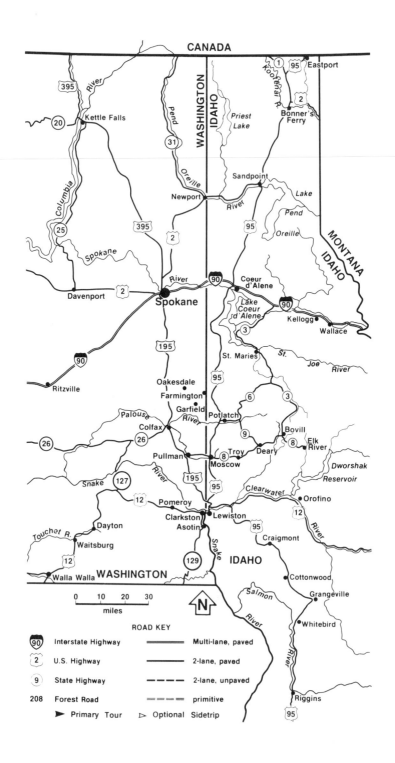

CANADA

WASHINGTON
IDAHO

395

River

Kootenai R.

1 95 Eastport

20 Kettle Falls

Pend

31

2 Bonner's Ferry

Priest Lake

MONTANA
IDAHO

Columbia

Oreille

River

Sandpoint

Lake

Newport

Pend

25

395

2

Spokane

95

Oreille

River

90 Coeur d'Alene

Davenport

2

Spokane

Lake Coeur rd'Alene

90

Kellogg

3

Wallace

90

195

Ritzville

St. Maries

95

St.

Joe

River

Oakesdale

Farmington

Palouse

Garfield

River

Colfax

26

26

Potlatch

6

3

9

Bovill

8

Elk River

Pullman

8 Troy

Moscow

Deary

Dworshak Reservoir

Snake

River

127

195

95

Clearwater

Orofino

12 Pomeroy

Clarkston
Asotin

Lewiston

12

River

Touchet R.

Dayton

95

Craigmont

Waitsburg

12

129

Snake

IDAHO

Walla Walla WASHINGTON

Cottonwood

Salmon

Grangeville

0 10 20 30
miles

N

River

Whitebird

River

ROAD KEY

90 Interstate Highway ———— Multi-lane, paved

2 U.S. Highway ——— 2-lane, paved

9 State Highway - - - - 2-lane, unpaved

208 Forest Road ==== primitive

► Primary Tour ▷ Optional Sidetrip

Riggins

95

UMBRELLA GUIDE TO
THE INLAND EMPIRE

by

Bill London

T.M.

UMBRELLA BOOKS

ISBN: 0-914143-26-3

Published by:

Umbrella Books
A Division of Harbor View Publications Group, Inc.
440 Tucker Ave., PO Box 1460
Friday Harbor, WA 98250-1460

CREDITS

Cover design:	Elizabeth Watson
Cover photo:	Randy Wells
Maps:	Tom Rice

Interior photos are by the author, except:

Wallace Depot Museum, by Betty Thiessen Meloy

Jackson Sundown, courtesy Nez Perce Historical Park

Virgil McCroskey, courtesy Latah County Historical Society

Bill Moreland, courtesy Bert Rusell

W.H. Cowles, courtesy Cowles Publishing

Bill London, by Charlie Powell

Table of Contents

Umbrella Guides to the Pacific Northwest

Jerome K. Miller, Series Editor

Umbrella Guide to Friday Harbor & San Juan Island

Umbrella Guide to Bicycling the Oregon Coast

Umbrella Guide to the Inland Empire

Umbrella Guide to Washington Lighthouses

Forthcoming Titles

Umbrella Guide to Glacier & Waterton National Parks

Umbrella Guide to Northwest Hot Springs

Umbrella Guide to San Juan Island Beaches

Umbrella Guide to Inland Empire Antique Stores

Umbrella Guide to Victoria B.C.

Praise for The Umbrella Guide Series

"Exploring the Northwest will be more enjoyable with the help of these guides. The excellent Umbrella Guide series offers in-depth coverage of areas and subjects that are unusual and offbeat — and interesting."

> Archie Satterfield, author of the *Seattle Guidebook* and former newspaper and magazine editor

This book identifies many interesting sites in the Inland Empire. Mountain trails, river banks, and old mines are great to visit, but readers must exercise considerable caution to avoid injury. It is particularly important that children be properly supervised. Please fasten your seat belts and observe every reasonable caution while driving.

Introduction

This guidebook covers the old Spokane-based Inland Empire. Though its boundaries are not officially defined, the Inland Empire includes North Idaho as far south as White Bird and the Salmon River, and Eastern Washington as far west as Kettle Falls and Walla Walla. This includes the Spokane metropolitan area, the mountains, valleys and fields of the Idaho Panhandle, and the desert-to-alpine variety of Eastern Washington.

The Inland Empire was originally a boosterish term given by early settlers to the area around Spokane. In 1883, Frank M. Dallam, a Spokane newspaper editor, described the Inland Empire as "an immense region of unlimited resources and possibilities that will in later years give subsistence and support to millions of human beings."

The same sense of openness and opportunity that attracted missionaries, miners, loggers, homesteaders and merchants to the Inland Empire remains today. It is an area filled with fascinating characters and magnificent countryside. I have tried to capture both in this guidebook.

The book is divided into thirteen chapters. Each chapter is an automobile and bicycle tour, complete with maps, mileages and plenty of roadside attractions, most of which are free. Each chapter provides a different perspective of the amazing diversity of the region. The Inland Empire has mines and miners, woods and loggers, farms and farmers, and plenty of oddballs that don't fit in any category. You will meet them all in the guidebook.

I included profiles of twenty individuals, some prominent historically, but most living and working in the area. They are real people and you are welcome to visit with them. They are friendly and approachable people, filled with the same independent spirit that pervades this open country.

The Inland Empire is one of the least-densely-populated parts of the Continental U.S. This region is equally remarkable for its variety. If you like deserts, they're available. If you prefer forests, there are plenty. Or how about a swimming beach, or a rocky crag, or a mountain lake? All are nearby.

All these tours can be completed in an hour or two. But each one can be savored in a journey of a day, or even a week. Take time to see the country and meet the people. If you budget an extra day, you'll eat more tree-ripened peaches, see more elk, or cool more toes in mountain lakes. No telling what you'll see or who you'll meet. If you find something particularly enjoyable, please write me at PO Box 8152, Moscow, Idaho 83843. I would like to hear from you.

Thanks. Have a great trip.

Bill London

DEDICATION

This book is dedicated to my beloved Gormleys, Gina and Willow, who are the reason for it all — and to Jim Prall, since together we took the day trip to Farmington that evolved into Chapter 1.

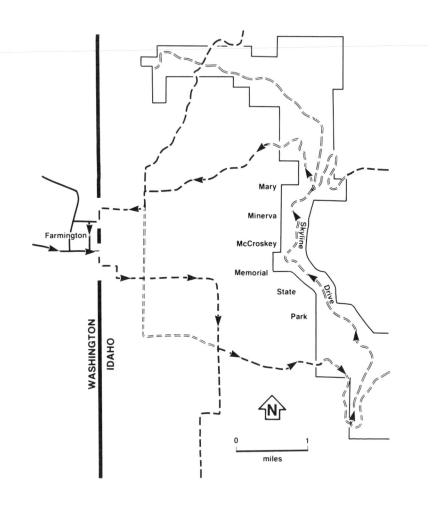

Mary

Minerva

McCroskey

Memorial

State

Park

Skyline

Drive

Farmington

WASHINGTON

IDAHO

N

0   1
miles

x

Chapter 1

FARMINGTON AND BEYOND

(16 miles)

Time: A minimum of one hour by automobile.

Services: This tour begins and ends at the small town of Farmington, Washington. Meals, gasoline, groceries, public restrooms and drinking water are available in Farmington. No other services or facilities are available along the tour.

Bicycles: This tour is ill-suited for most bicyclists. The road is narrow and winding throughout, and very steep in some portions. No services are provided anywhere except at the beginning and end of this loop tour. The road is dirt along the entire tour. Experienced riders on mountain bikes would enjoy the beautiful vistas along this route, but pedal with care.

Wheelchairs: Unless otherwise noted, the facilities listed in this chapter are wheelchair accessible.

This short tour begins and ends in Farmington, a small agricultural community on the Washington/Idaho border. A sixteen-mile dirt road leaves Farmington, heads into the Idaho foothills to the east, winds to the crest of the ridge above the town and then returns. The road is very narrow and winding, and not well-maintained, but it is passable to all vehicles except large RVs. Expect some dust, but very little traffic.

1

Farmington is located off Washington Highway 27, about forty miles north of Lewiston, Idaho, and fifty miles south of Spokane. Five miles north of Garfield or eight miles south of Oakesdale, a two-lane paved road marked as the Farmington Road heads east from Highway 27. Farmington is located five miles from Highway 27 on this road. In Farmington, the road becomes Washington Street.

Farmington

The town of Farmington, first settled in 1870, was one of the first communities on the Palouse. The Palouse is the name given to that area of rolling hills located south of Spokane and north of the Snake River in North Idaho and Eastern Washington. The Palouse hills have unusual dune-like shapes, steep on their northeast sides, with long gradual slopes to the southwest. The shape is a result of their origin. The hills were created by years of wind-blown dust and volcanic ash from the southwest. The prevailing winds up the Columbia River valley over the last several million years dropped finely-powdered dust and clay on the area to build the hills. This fertile and productive soil is known as loess (pronounced luss) because of its wind-blown origin. The Palouse hills, except for the steepest slopes, are now planted to grains, like wheat and barley, and to legumes, like lentils and peas.

The name Palouse (pronounced pah-LOOSE) is assumed by many to have come from the word left by the French trappers who first visited the area. They called it "pelouse," meaning grass-covered hills. A more likely source is the name of the local tribe's main village located at the confluence of the Snake and Palouse Rivers. The village, called "Palus," meant "something sticking down in the water," such as the large rock the Indians believed was the solidified heart of the Beaver. From whatever source, the name has been retained by the area's largest river, one of its first towns, the tribe which originally inhabited the area, and by the spotted horses bred by the Nez Perce Indians (the "palousies" or Appaloosa).

The first white settlers were ranchers drawn by the abundant feed for their animals. The nearby hills – the destination of this loop tour – offered plenty of wood for building and burning. Their water needs were easily satisfied by an artesian well in Farmington.

2

Town historian Laurence Wright says the water from that artesian well filled a horse-watering trough for many years. Later, the well was capped to provide the town's water source. Wright, the author of *Farmington: A Pictorial History*, explained that the town was originally named Pine Creek, and that it was not until 1888 that it was incorporated as Farmington.

The railroad came to Farmington in 1886. The town was the end of the line from the Palouse's largest city, Colfax. A locomotive turntable and roundhouse were built in Farmington, and the population peaked at 1,200 in 1888. Two years later, however, the rail line was extended and the roundhouse was moved to nearby Tekoa, Washington. The population dropped steadily from that point, until now about one-hundred people live in Farmington.

Unlike many slowly withering rural communities in the Inland Empire, Farmington has an obvious sense of community pride. The few empty buildings are clean and well kept. Large, well-maintained parks fill several lots. The old Masonic Hall has been resurrected as a community center. The streets are wide, the houses attractive, and the entire town has a classic Norman Rockwell feel to it.

Upon entering Farmington, turn left on First Street, at the town's only gas station/convenience store, to find the "downtown" business section. Turn right at the next intersection, Main Street. The Bank of Farmington, an amazingly tiny, but perfectly functional financial institution, is on the left at the corner of Main and First. Ahead is an old horse-drawn road grader left on display. On the right, down Main Street, is the town's other commercial establishment, the Frying Pan Cafe, plus the post office, community center, and town park. The cafe and bank are not wheelchair accessible.

The park at Second and Main provides drinking water and restrooms, plus horseshoe pits, a tennis court, a lovely shaded picnic area, plenty of barbeque grills, and a children's play area, all available at no charge. A small tower at the corner of the park houses a bell and some old firefighting equipment.

Frying Pan Cafe

When Dick and Jeannie Dando bought the Farmington Inn, it was just another watering hole, the only one in town. They changed the name to the Frying Pan Cafe, to acknowledge Jeannie's unusual hobby. She was the "Frying Pan Lady." She collected frying pans, painted them black, and added caricatures to the bottoms of the pans. Before her death, more than six-hundred painted frying pans covered the walls of the cafe.

Jeannie Dando used pans of all sizes and materials for her art. After painting the pans black, she traced cartoon designs, often from the pages of coloring books, onto the flat surface. She then chose the colors and did the painting herself.

Many pans came from friends, especially from a man who made regular pilgrimages to Spokane's thrift shops and rummage sales for them. Jeannie and Dick also cruised the local sales. "When they saw us coming at rummage sales, they'd all say: Well, here comes the Frying Pan Lady, and pull out a box of frying pans — and I'd be out two bucks," Dick Dando recalled.

When Jeannie died in 1987, Dick had trouble keeping the business open without her. Early in 1989, Mary Beauchman and Judy Frey bought the cafe. Several hundred of Jeannie's gaily decorated pans were included in the sale, and still hang on the walls. Other pans went to friends and relatives or to storage — except for Jeannie's first creation. The small pan Jeannie painted in 1979 to launch her hobby was saved for a fitting monument. It will be placed, painted side out, in the concrete of the memorial stone at her grave. Below it will be inscribed: Frying Pan Lady, Jeannie D. Dando.

The Frying Pan Cafe is open daily, on Main Street in Farmington. The building is not wheelchair accessible. The address is PO Box 154, Farmington, WA 98128, (509) 287-2005.

Mary Beauchmon and Judy Frey.

To continue the tour, turn right on Second Street and then left onto Washington Street at the next intersection. Continue ahead, across the railroad tracks, toward the forested hills east of town. Those hills are part of Idaho's Mary Minerva McCroskey State Park. McCroskey Park includes 5,200 acres of timberland and meadow along the east-west ridge from the foothills of the Bitterroot Mountains in Idaho into the Palouse. Skyline Drive, a twenty-five-mile-long dirt road, winds along the ridge from Idaho Highway 95 north of Potlatch to Farmington. Bridging of the two ecological zones within the park — the forest and the grassland — creates a remarkable diversity of plant communities there. Eleven habitat types, from the wet cedar forest to the dry south-facing grassy slopes, are found in McCroskey Park. This ecological diversity is unique among Idaho parks.

To The Hill of Illusion

The tour follows Washington Street east of Farmington. At the edge of town, the road turns to dirt and crosses the railroad tracks. Within one-hundre yards, the road crosses the state boundary into Idaho. The border is unmarked, and for many practical purposes does not exist. The cove of agricultural land ahead is surrounded by forested mountains and has no paved access into the rest of Idaho.

The road winds occasionally after it leaves Farmington, passing a few farms. At the first intersection, 1 1/4 miles from Farmington, continue straight ahead. One mile further, turn right at the T junction. One mile past the T junction, in a small grove of trees, turn left onto Pine Creek Road. The small farmhouse on the right at that intersection is marked with a mailbox with Floyd Palmer's name on it.

The road now parallels Pine Creek east into the mountains. One mile ahead, at a single pine tree, a narrow farmer's road crosses. Remain on the main road ahead, which curves slightly to the left. One quarter-mile farther, at the crest of the small hill, stop by the grove of five pine trees. Ahead is the Hill of Illusion.

This is an optical illusion. For the next hundred yards, the road appears to descend. Perhaps due to the placement of the road at the edge of the forested hills above, or possibly because of the way the adjacent plowed fields slope away, the road definitely appears to go downhill. The road, in fact, goes uphill at a slight angle. Vehicles will appear to coast uphill at the Hill of Illusion.

Those who wish to test the direction of the slope can bring a large ball, like an inflatable beach ball, to see which way the ball rolls when placed on the roadway. Even a plumb bob or level will reveal the actual direction of slope.

The tour continues up the road ahead, past the curve and into the trees. The road ahead is narrow and passing turnouts are few, but traffic is light on this route. Drive carefully and slowly. As the roadway climbs into the forest, the tour enters McCroskey Park.

Mary Minerva McCroskey State Park

Two miles past the Hill of Illusion, the road suddenly reaches the crest. There is a small overlook area ahead at the ridgetop, but a better and larger viewpoint is adjacent to the intersection ahead.

Follow the main road as it curves left toward the ridgetop. Fifty feet away is an intersection. Turn left onto Skyline Drive through McCroskey Park. An overlook site is adjacent to this intersection.

This tour continues on Skyline Drive to the west. Beautiful views of the Palouse to the left are presented whenever there is an opening in the trees. Virgil McCroskey's other gift mountain, Steptoe Butte, is the pointed volcano-like peak about twenty miles west.

Skyline Drive crosses two small water sources, the first about three-quarters of a mile from the ridgetop intersection and the second about one-quarter mile further. Both springs are located on the right side of the road, and both have been developed with small cement dams to create tiny ponds for wildlife watering. The ferns and forget-me-nots that grow around those springs are lush and lovely, but the water is not safe to drink.

The question of who built the two cement catch dams is answered by the inscription left at the second dam. In the center of the dam, note the initials "VTM" and the year "64." Virgil T. McCroskey poured this cement in 1964, when he was 88 years old.

The tour continues ahead. The ecological changes continue as well, as the wetter forest of cedar and fir gives way to the dry Ponderosa Pine forest and then finally to grassland. The grassland provides many beautiful views. About two and one-half miles past the second cement catch dam, the road leaves the trees. The grassy knob offers plenty of flat spots for picnics complete with 360-degree views. Behind this knob are the forested hills of Idaho and ahead are the grainfields of the

Virgil McCroskey, Parkmaster

Virgil T. McCroskey was a pioneer conservationist. He was profoundly influenced by the state park movement of the 1930's and 1940's, a nationwide crusade to establish small parks. Long before the preservation ethic arose in the Inland Empire, he established two state parks in this region.

From 1899 to 1920, McCroskey was a pharmacist. At age forty-four, he retired, sold the Elk Drug Store in Colfax, Washington, and moved to the family homestead in nearby Oakesdale. For the next twenty years he travelled worldwide, returning periodically to beautify his estate with imported plants. In his sixth decade of life, McCroskey sold the home to finance his vision of local parks in the Palouse.

His first successful acquisition was Steptoe Butte. He bought forty acres including the summit, the spiralling roadway to the top, and an eighty-acre picnic area at the base. In 1946, he gave it to the Washington Department of Parks "for the enjoyment of all the people forever and ever."

In 1939, he started his most ambitious project, McCroskey State Park in Idaho. By 1946, he purchased 650 acres of forest and meadow, and constructed seven miles of roadway along one of the forested ridges that snake into the Palouse grainfields. He called it Skyline Drive.

Five years later, he offered the state of Idaho a two-thousand acre park and a nearly-complete twenty-five-mile ridgetop road. The Idaho Legislature refused his gift, even though the state only had two parks. McCroskey tried again in 1953, when he offered 2,800 acres and pledged $500 annually for fifteen years for park maintenance. Again he was refused. Perhaps the Idaho Legislature was mystified by his generosity. Nobody, before or since, had purchased land in Idaho specifically to create a state park. He then directed a state-wide public relations campaign to pressure the legislature into accepting his

8

 park the third time in 1955, it had grown to 4,400 acres. Mc-Croskey promised to maintain the parkland himself for fifteen years, and establish a trust fund for its perpetual maintenance. The legislature finally accepted his offer, and Governor Robert Smylie signed the legislation establishing Mary Minerva McCroskey State Park. The park was named for Virgil's mother, in honor of the pioneer women of the region.

Virgil McCroskey was seventy-nine when Idaho accepted his pledge to maintain the park for fifteen years, and he kept his word. Throughout the Palouse, people still speak of his dedication, and his ability to motivate others to help him plant bushes, create picnic areas, and clear trails. He died on September 14, 1970 — almost ninety-four years old — after finishing his fifteen-year commitment at McCroskey State Park.

After his death, the Idaho Parks and Recreation Department allowed the park to deteriorate. Brush filled the trails and the picnic tables disintegrated. A recent campaign by friends and relatives of Virgil McCroskey pressured the department to honor its old committment. The Parks Department now uses the earnings from McCroskey's trust fund for park maintenance, instead of adding the money to their general fund. McCroskey Park will remain a primitive park with few conveniences, as Virgil McCroskey suggested. But, in keeping with his wishes, the trails and tables he built will be restored.

9

Palouse country. Forested ridges mix and mingle with the plowed fields. It is lovely.

The tour continues ahead, and Skyline Drive dips back into the trees. One-half mile ahead, on the left, is a picnic table, the only one now in the park. This table is in the forest, and has no view. There are no restrooms or drinking water.

About 1 1/4 miles past the open grassy knob, the road forks. Skyline Drive, and this tour, continue to the left. Another quarter-mile ahead, the road forks again. Turn left toward Farmington. Within a mile and one-half, the road enters the cultivated grainfields again. Three miles from the fork, the road ends at a T junction. Turn left. The road enters Farmington about one and one-half miles past the T junction. Turn right at Washington Street to return to Highway 27.

The Farmington loop is complete. Past the Hill of Illusion and along Skyline Drive, this tour has sampled both the Palouse and the forest in one of the loveliest places in the Inland Empire.

Chapter 2

ACROSS THE DAMMED SNAKE

(28 miles)

Time: A minimum of forty-five minutes by automobile.

Services: All services are available in Pullman. Restrooms and drinking water also are available in Klemgard Park, Boyer Park, the Lower Granite Dam Visitor Center, and Illia Landing.

Bicycles: This tour is well-suited for bicycles. The roadways are paved and offer wide shoulders along virtually the entire route. Expect a steep descent to the Snake River.

Wheelchairs: This tour is well-suited for wheelchairs. Many of the vistas are visible from inside vehicles. Unless otherwise indicated, the facilites described in this chapter are wheelchair accessible.

From Pullman, Washington, the tour descends about two-thousand feet to the Snake River. The tour leaves the cultivated rolling hills of the Palouse Country to finish at the recreational mecca of the river. The tour crosses the Snake River on a road on top of Lower Granite Dam.

From The Palouse To The Snake

This tour begins in Pullman, in southeastern Washington, about eighty miles south of Spokane. At 24,000 population, Pullman is the

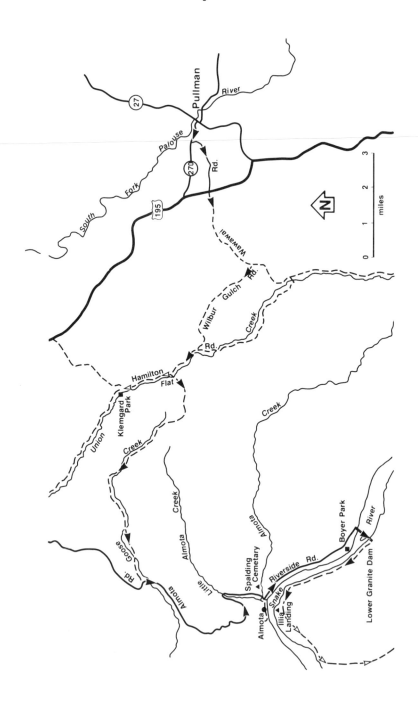

What to Do at WSU

Washington State University in Pullman is the biggest university in the Inland Empire. The university's initials, WSU, are pronounced locally as Wah-ZOO. Six free museums on campus house a wide variety of exhibits and collections. Call to verify that they are open, especially during university holidays.

The Ownbey Herbarium in Heald Hall displays dried specimens of more than 300,000 evergreens, ferns, and mosses. (509) 335-3250.

The Museum of Art at the Fine Art Center offers a small permanent collection and rotating exhibits. (509) 335-1910.

The Anthropology Museum in Johnson Tower displays Indian basketry, Big Foot lore, and New Guinea tribal artifacts. (509) 335-3936.

The Mycological Herbarium in Johnson Hall contains thousands of mushroom and fungi specimens. (509) 335-9541.

The Jacklin Collection in the Physical Sciences Building includes petrified wood, fluorescent minerals, dinosaur bones and other rocks. (509) 335-7014.

The James Entomological Museum in Johnson Hall houses about one million insect specimens. (509) 335-3394.

largest city in Whitman County and the home of Washington State University. In 1876, the town was established, and named Three Forks, for the creeks that meet there to form the South Fork of the Palouse River. On July 4, 1881, the town was renamed in honor of the maker of the pullman railroad car to attract railroads and businesses to the area. The effort had little success, but a later land donation persuaded the state to establish a university there. The university has become the town's economic mainstay.

See page 174 for the Cougar Creamery

From downtown Pullman, follow Highway 270 (Davis Way) toward Colfax and Spokane. The road rises quickly out of the valley of the South Fork of the Palouse River as it leaves the town. About three-quarters of a mile from downtown Pullman, turn left on Wawawai Road (pronounced wah-wah-WHY, or even wah-WHY). The junction is clearly marked with signs toward Almota, Wawawai, and Klemgard Park.

Wawawai Road immediately enters the grainfields characteristic of this region. This section of Eastern Washington and North Idaho is filled with rolling dune-shaped hills that were once covered with tall grasses, but which are now devoted to wheat, barley, lentils, dry peas, and the yellow-flowered rapeseed. The region is known locally as the Palouse. The region is very productive agriculturally. Visually, the contrast of the checkerboard fields and the undulating landscape is delightful. (More information on the Palouse region is in Chapter 1.)

Follow Wawawai Road ahead. Cross Highway 195 three miles from Pullman, and continue on Wawawai Road. At the junction five miles from Pullman, turn right onto Wilbur Gulch Road. Follow the signs to Almota. The junction is clearly marked.

At all the road cuts along the route, note the black rock that underlays the loess soil. This is basalt, which repeatedly oozed out as molten material from cracks in the earth, creating this layered rock. More information on basalt is contained in Chapter 13. More of the layers will be visible as the tour continues and as the erosive power of the river reveals more of them.

Ten miles from Pullman, at the intersection of Hamilton Road and Wilbur Gulch Road, follow Wilbur Gulch Road to the left, toward Almota. The intersection is clearly marked.

Optional Sidetrip To Klemgard Park

To visit Klemgard Park, continue straight ahead on Hamilton Road at the Wilbur Gulch Road junction. The road enters a rarity in the Palouse, a forested valley. Ponderosa Pines cling to the wet, north-facing side of the valley, while exposed basalt cliffs and dry-climate vegetation cover the south-facing slope.

About one and one-half miles from the Wilbur Gulch Road junction, turn left off Hamilton Road onto Union Flat Road. This intersection is marked with a sign to Klemgard Park. One mile from the Hamilton Road intersection, note Klemgard Park on the left. This county park offers grassy picnic sites and a natural forested area. Union Flat Creek bisects the park. A one-mile-long self-guided interpretive trail focuses on both the natural and historical aspects of the area. The park is open for day-use only at no charge. Playground facilities, a large picnic shelter, a baseball field, horseshoe pits, and volleyball courts are provided. For more information, contact the Whitman County Parks Department, 101 N. Main, Colfax WA 99111, (509) 397-4622.

To return to the tour, retrace this route to the Wilbur Gulch and Hamilton Road junction.

Down To The River

After turning south toward Almota on Wilbur Gulch Road, the road slowly loses elevation as it begins a two-thousand-foot drop to the bottom of the Snake River canyon. Seven miles past the Wilbur Gulch and Hamilton Road intersection, turn left onto Almota Road, toward Almota. This intersection is clearly marked. The road begins to descend steeply, with sections of nine percent grade ahead. The road is paved and passable to all vehicles.

Beautiful views of the Snake River canyon accompany the turns of this road. Note the increasing numbers of basalt layers exposed on the canyon walls as the valley deepens. This is desert country. It is warm and summerish here when the Palouse above is shivering in early spring. Poison ivy and rattlesnakes thrive in this warm climate, so take suitable precautions.

Fourteen miles from the Wilbur Gulch and Hamilton Road intersection, the tour reaches the Snake River at the village of Almota. At the river, turn left toward Boyer Park.

Almota once thrived as a steamboat stop and a ford and ferry crossing of the river. An ancient Indian pathway, known as the Red Wolf Trail, later renamed the Stevens Trail (see Chapter 11), crossed the river here and followed the present roadway up to the Palouse Country. The Lewis and Clark Expedition floated to Almota from their encampment at Tsceminicum (see Chapter 12) and spent the night of October 11, 1805, at the mouth of Almota Creek. At one time, Almota was a prosperous town with hotels and warehouses. One of the hotel owners was Henry H. Spalding, son of the pioneer missionaries Henry and Eliza Spalding (see Chapter 13).

Optional Sidetrip To Spalding Cemetery

To visit the Spalding cemetery, park at the intersection where the dirt road meets Almota Road, near the railroad bridge. Pull off to the left about twenty yards before you reach the bridge. Park adjacent to Almota Road, without driving through either gate.

A quarter-mile trek across private property is required to reach the cemetery at the top of the hill. Sturdy shoes are essential. Tall boots and long pants are preferred to shed burrs and to protect legs from rattlesnakes.

This property is part of a huge cattle ranch owned by Larry Hickman of Colfax. He allows people to cross his property to reach the cemetery as long as they observe two rules. First, do not drive past the gates, and second, never leave a gate open. Please follow his wishes.

After parking at the entrance to the dirt road, walk through the green metal gate ahead and continue fifty yards on the dirt road that parallels Almota Creek. Then, turn left up a narrower dirt road that leads uphill to a cattle feeding area. Go through the brown metal gate near the tree. Twenty yards beyond the second gate, note the fenced area, about seventy-five yards away, at the top of the hill to the left. That is the Spalding Cemetery.

There is no trail to the cemetary, so visitors must walk through the field. The cemetery is surrounded by a fairly new barbed-wire fence, and within that, an old wrought-iron fence. The gate through the wrought-iron fence opens easily. Inside are the graves of Henry H. Spalding (born at Lapwai in 1839 and died at Almota in 1898), his wife, Mary C. Spalding (1854 to 1941), and two of their children, Effie Edith and Harry. Both of the Spalding's children died in infancy. Effie was born in March of 1879 and died the following January. Harry was born in June of 1877 and died in October of 1878.

The view from the cemetery, of the river and the canyon, is worth the walk. The canyon looks much as it did in Spalding's time. The dam is not visible, and the river appears to be free-flowing.

To continue the tour, walk back to the vehicle and continue on Almota Road to the river. Turn left (east) on Riverside Road toward Lower Granite Dam and Boyer Park.

Henry H. Spalding was the first male born to American citizens in the Pacific Northwest. He is buried, with his wife and two of their children, near Almota. A visit to the family graveyard nearby is well worth the short walk.

Boyer Park

Boyer Park is on the right, one and one-half miles from Almota on Riverside Road. Boyer is an oasis. In the summer, it provides the only green grass in the canyon. This forty-acre park is a recreationalists' paradise. It's open year-round to accommodate boaters, anglers, swimmers, and hikers. The park offers an enclosed swimming area, a sandy beach, picnic facilities, full hookup campsites, laundry facilities, showers, a convenience store and a restaurant. The marina provides dockside gasoline, a marine dump station, and a free launch ramp. Day use is free. Contact Boyer Park and Marina, Rt. 3, Box 69, Colfax, WA 99111, (509) 397-3208.

Avoiding Death by Turbine Blades

About fifteen percent of the young steelhead and salmon were killed as they swam downstream through the turbine blades at the dams on the Columbia/Snake River system. The population decline in the smolts (the name given the young fish) became obvious in the late 1960s when there were only four dams on the Columbia. Since four more dams were planned for the mid-1970s, something had to be done.

In 1968, the US Army Corps of Engineers began Operation Fish Run, the most ambitious and successful juvenile fish transport system in the US. The smolts were diverted from the turbines by a system of screens, which led them to holding tanks. Tank trucks, and later a fleet of barges, carried the fish to a site below Bonneville Dam near Portland, thereby avoiding the dangerous turbines.

The smolt collection site, near Lower Granite Dam's Visitor Center, is open to visitors. It is open only when the smolts migrate downstream, usually from March to July. The tours are free, but call ahead to make reservations for a guided tour. The tour includes the barges, holding tanks, and inspection area, where a small percentage of the smolts are marked, counted, weighed and sorted before transporting. The tour is not wheelchair accessible. Contact the US Army Corps of Engineers, Lower Granite Dam Resources Office, Rt. 3, Box 54, Pomeroy, WA, 99347 (509) 843-1493.

Lower Granite Dam

Continue past Boyer Park two miles to Lower Granite Dam. This dam, the eighth and uppermost on the Columbia/Snake River system, was completed in 1975. The tour continues across the top of the dam. The roadway is winding and narrow, so drive with care. The road over the dam closes between 10 P.M. and 6 A.M. The dam is wide enough to provide some parking places to view the canyon or watch boats pass through the locks. The locks are huge concrete boxes with doors at each end that fill or empty with water to raise or lower boats moored inside. The lock at Lower Granite is gigantic: 675 feet long and eighty-six feet wide, filled with forty-six million gallons of water, and able to lift or lower boats more than one-hundred feet.

The lock at Lower Granite is at the north end of the dam, near Boyer Park. Park near the lock and walk to the cement wall that surrounds it. When boats going downstream enter the lock, their decks are about ten feet below the roadway. The water level drops more than one hundred feet in about ten minutes. After the 388-ton doors open, the boats continue their downstream voyage. It's great entertainment.

After crossing the Snake, turn right and continue down the ramp. At the bottom of the ramp, before the Operation Fish Run building, turn right on the paved entranceway to the Lower Granite Dam Visitor Center. The center is open daily at no charge. Displays of local history and Native American culture are provided, but the highlight is the fish-viewing room. Visitors get close-up views of three- and four-foot long salmon and steelhead, and many smaller fish. Contact the US Army Corps of Engineers, Lower Granite Dam Project, Rt. 3, Box 54, Pomeroy, WA 99347, (509) 843-1493.

To The Dunes

Continue the tour by following Riverside Road toward Pomeroy. The road parallels the Snake River and provides a great view of the canyon and Boyer Park on the opposite bank.

Illia Landing is three miles from the visitor center. A launch ramp, boat dock, picnic tables, grills, and vault toilets are provided. Drinking water is not available here.

One mile past Illia Landing, two large parking lots on the right provide entry to the Dunes. The Dunes is the local name for the huge sandy beach that stretches for about a mile along the south bank of the Snake. It is an undeveloped natural area, open for day use only, at no charge. Drinking water is not available here. Several vault toilets are near the parking lots. For most of its length, the sand is more than one hundred yards wide, so there are plenty of places for picnics, swimming, and sunbathing. The Dunes is a favorite stop for local teens and university students. No motorized vehicles are allowed on the Dunes.

The road continues to Pomeroy, rising quickly out of the canyon. The river canyon displays long, horizontal ribbons of basalt rock on the walls. After a short season of green grass and wildflowers in the early spring, the canyon dries to brown. The blue water of the Snake contrasts invitingly with the dark walls of the canyon. The tour ends here. Continue ahead to Pomeroy or return to the Palouse.

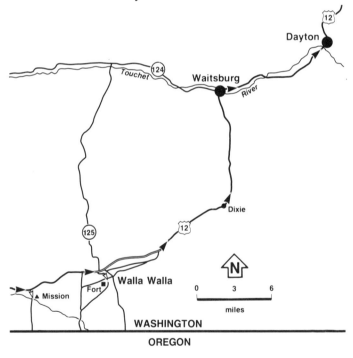

The Cradle of the Inland Empire.

Chapter 3

THE CRADLE OF

INLAND EMPIRE HISTORY

(37 miles)

Time: A minimum of forty-five minutes by automobile.

Services: Drinking water and restrooms are available at the Whitman Mission, at the start of the tour, and at the Lewis and Clark Trail State Park midway between Waitsburg and Dayton. In addition, all services are offered at Walla Walla, Dixie, Waitsburg and Dayton.

Bicycles: This tour is well-suited to bicyclists. The route is mostly two-lane paved road, often with wide shoulders. The exception is a short stretch of freeway skirting Walla Walla. That section, which is off limits to non-motorized traffic, can be bypassed easily on the old highway. The bypass is clearly marked as Business Highway 12. Restrooms and drinking water are available at regular intervals. No steep grades are found along this tour.

Wheelchairs: Unless otherwise indicated, all of the places described in this chapter are wheelchair accessible.

Walla Walla is where it all started. The fertile plain, where three creeks meet the Walla Walla River, became the home of Marcus and Narcissa Whitman in 1836. The Whitmans were the first American

The Whitmans, The First Family

The Whitmans and Spaldings were the first U.S. families to cross the Rockies into the Inland Empire. They came as missionaries to the Indians. The Spaldings settled in Lapwai, among the Nez Perce. (Their history is detailed in Chapter 13.)

Marcus and Narcissa Whitman came to a place of abundant water and fertile pasture seven miles west of Walla Walla, now known as the Whitman Mission National Historic Site. Their settlement, the only one in present Eastern Washington, was the site of many military and civilian "firsts."

No photographs remain of the Whitman family. Marcus was described as six feet tall, strong and hardworking. Visitors noted that Narcissa was energetic, slight, and attractive. Both were born in New York state, Marcus in 1802 and Narcissa in 1808. Marcus became a doctor in 1825, and ten years later decided to be a medical missionary. After their wedding on February 18, 1836, the service closed with the hymn "Yes, My Native Land! I Love Thee." The obvious reference to their dangerous departure into the unknown was too much for the congregation. One after another, everyone there broke down into sobs. At the end of the song, contemporary accounts recall, only Narcissa's voice could be heard. Their trip to the wilderness was their honeymoon.

The Whitmans established their mission at Waiilatpu ("the place of the people of the rye grass") in 1836. By 1839, fields of grain were planted, a millpond and grist mill were in operation and their first crude shacks were replaced with substantial buildings. By 1842, they sold flour and produce to the first settlers taking the Oregon Trail west. Though the Trail later took the shortcut through what is now Pendleton, Oregon, thousands of pioneers stopped at the Whitman Mission, since it was the only sign of civilization for hundreds of miles.

Narcissa wrote to her relatives about the appeal of the mission to travelers. In a letter dated October 9, 1844, she wrote:

Here we are, one family alone, a way mark, as it were, or center post, about which the multitudes will or must gather this winter. And these we must feed and warm to the extent of our powers.

Their only child, Alice Clarisse, was born on March 14, 1837. Alice was the first child born to American citizens in the Pacific Northwest. Tragically, Alice drowned two years later. The Whitmans had plenty of children to raise, however. They adopted four children, the offspring of Indian women and American trappers and adventurers. Seven orphaned children of the Seger family also were placed in their care.

On November 29, 1847, a group of Cayuse Indians came to kill the Whitmans. Increasing numbers of settlers and a measles epidemic angered the Indians. Seventy-four people lived at the mission, occupying every outbuilding. Thirteen people, including both Whitmans, were killed and fifty were captured. The others escaped in the confusion. After one month, the captives were ransomed for blankets, shirts, and guns. For several years, up to five-hundred volunteers from Oregon Territory searched for the guilty Cayuse, ultimately hanging five men for the crime.

Many others followed the Whitmans into the Walla Walla area, but they were the first family, and without them the history of the Inland Empire would have been very different.

family to settle in what is now Eastern Washington, and their daughter was the first child born to US citizens in the Pacific Northwest. Others settled on the land around the Whitman Mission, and the Walla Walla area became the only permanent population center for hundreds of miles. It was a way station on the original route of the Oregon Trail. Many assumed it would become the largest city in the Northwest.

When the Washington Territory was created in 1853, the town was selected as the seat of Walla Walla County—an area including all of present-day Eastern Washington, plus most of Idaho and western Montana. At the Great Treaty Council of 1855, in Walla Walla, Territorial Governor Isaac Stevens met with five-thousand Indians and secured the rights to most of the Inland Empire for American settlers. Fort Walla Walla was established in 1859, and the fort was immediately the hub of a system of trails and roads throughout the Inland Empire, including the Mullan Road to Montana.

Though Walla Walla was the first settlement, it is no longer the population center or the commercial hub of the Inland Empire. That title has shifted to Spokane. But Walla Walla was the cradle, the place where American settlers first arrived with their brand of civilization.

The Whitman Mission

The tour starts on Highway 12, about five miles east of Lowden and seven miles west of Walla Walla in southeastern Washington. Turn south on Swegle Road. The intersection is clearly marked. Drive about one-half mile to the entrance of the Whitman Mission.

Ninety-eight acres surrounding the original Whitman home was preserved as the Whitman Mission National Historic Site in 1962. The Visitor Center is an appropriate place to begin this historic tour. A free ten-minute slide show, explaining the history of the area, the local tribes and the Whitman family, is offered every half hour. In addition, several large display areas exhibit artifacts from those early days. A grassy picnic area, complete with drinking water and restrooms is available.

Two must-see walking trails leave from the Visitor Center. One winds around the original site of the mission, the Whitman's home, the blacksmith shop, the grist mill, and the millpond. The pathway also crosses a restored section of the Oregon Trail. This self-guided loop trail is paved and about one-eighth of a mile long.

The second trail is longer, about one-quarter mile long, and steep where it winds to the top of the small hill where the Whitman Memorial is located. The beautiful view of the valley and the entire mission site justifies the short climb. This trail is paved.

The Mission is open daily from 8 A.M. to 6 P.M. in the summer and from 8 A.M. to 4:30 P.M. in the winter. A one-dollar admission fee per adult (or three-dollars per family) is charged. Children under sixteen and seniors over sixty are admitted free. For more information, contact Whitman Mission National Historic Site, Rt. 2, Walla Walla, WA 99362, (509) 522-6360 or (509) 529-2761.

Visiting Historic Fort Walla Walla

Fort Walla Walla was open from 1859 to 1910, and served as the focus of permanent settlement in the valley. Most of Walla Walla's historic sites are clustered on the original square mile of the fort. The fort complex is on the southwest corner of town, near the intersection of Myra Road and Rose Avenue.

The Fort Walla Walla Museum focuses on the pioneer life and agricultural history of the area. The Pioneer Village contains fourteen buildings, including homes, schoolhouses, shops and a railroad station. The buildings were brought to this location by the society which operates the museum. The museum includes five huge exhibit buildings with a fine collection of horse- and mule-drawn farming equipment. The museum is open daily, except Monday, during the summer. Admission is two dollars for those thirteen or older, and one dollar for children over six.

The Fort Walla Walla Military Cemetery is adjacent to the museum. Soldiers who died in Nineteenth Century Indian wars are buried there. The trees on the cemetery grounds are huge, and the cemetery is a pleasant place to walk.

In 1922, Fort Walla Walla became the Veterans Administration Medical Center. Fifteen of the original fort buildings are used by the Medical Center. Some were constructed in 1858 using adobe walls later covered with lumber. Free guided tours of the Medical Center are offered on weekdays. To arrange a tour, contact the Office of Public Affairs, Veterans Administration Medical Center, 77 Wainwright Drive, Walla Walla, WA 99362, (509) 525-5200.

Walla Walla

To continue the tour, return to Highway 12 and head east toward Walla Walla. The soil and climate of the area are still very productive, just as in Marcus Whitman's day. Fields on both sides of the highway are planted to grains, grapes, and row crops, especially onions—the famed Walla Walla Sweet Onions. Walla Walla was the Indian name for the valley. It translates as, "the place of many waters."

Seven miles from the Whitman Mission junction, the highway enters Walla Walla, now a city of 26,000. A good place to begin a visit is at the Chamber of Commerce. The Chamber offers maps of the town and the surrounding area, as well as information about accommodations and points of interest. Due to a recent fire, their new location is uncertain. Contact the Chamber through PO Box 644, Walla Walla, WA 99362, (509) 525-0850.

The local office of the US Forest Service is the best source for information about recreation in the Blue Mountains to the south of Walla Walla. Contact the US Forest Service, Walla Walla Ranger District, 1415 W Rose, Walla Walla, WA 99362, (509) 522-6290.

With some remarkable foresight, the founders of Walla Walla placed plenty of wonderful parks throughout the town. The best is fifty-eight-acre Pioneer Park, which is dominated by huge sycamore trees with beautiful low-hanging branches ideal for children's play. Squirrels, crows, and seagulls compete for handouts. Hundreds of exotic birds are housed in large cages at the aviary at the park. A large pond filled with ducks and geese, picnic areas, restrooms, drinking water, a rose garden, and a swimming pool also are provided. The park was designed by the famed landscape architect, John C. Olmstead, and it is indeed one of the loveliest in the region.

There is no admission charge to Pioneer Park or to the aviary. Pioneer Park is on Alder Street between Division and Roosevelt. For more information about this or other parks, contact the Walla Walla Parks and Recreation Department, City Hall, Third and Rose Streets, Walla Walla, WA 99362, (509) 527-4527.

Walla Walla Wine Tasting

The mild climate of the area is ideal for growing wine grapes. Many believe that viniculture will diversify and strengthen the local economy and provide enjoyable places to relax with samples of local wines. The five wineries offer free wine tasting and sales for off-premises consumption.

L'Ecole No 41 Winery, PO Box 111, Lowden, WA 99360, (509) 525-0940, open daily.

It is on Highway 12, about twelve miles west of Walla Walla, in the old Lowden Grade School. Entering Lowden from Walla Walla, L'Ecole is the first large building on the right.

Woodward Canyon Winery, Rt. 1, Box 387, Lowden, WA 99360, (509) 525-4129, open daily in the afternoons.

The winery is about 500 feet west of the L'Ecole Winery.

Biscuit Ridge Winery, Biscuit Ridge Road, Dixie, WA 99329, (509) 529-4986, open daily from 9 A.M. to 5 P.M.

Turn south from Highway 12 in Dixie onto Biscuit Ridge Road. The turn is well marked. Follow the road for three-quarters of a mile. The winery is on the right.

Leonetti Cellars, 1321 School Avenue, Walla Walla, WA 99362, (509) 525-1428, open by appointment only.

The directions are given over the phone.

Waterbrook Winery, Box 46, MacDonald Road, Walla Walla, WA 99362, (509) 522-1918, open by appointment only.

It is on MacDonald Road, which crosses Highway 12 about ten miles west of Walla Walla and about 1 1/2 miles east of Lowden. Turn south onto MacDonald Road. About two miles from the highway, the winery is on the right.

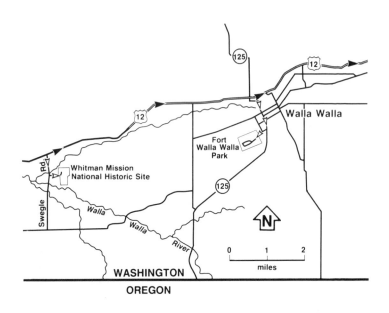

Walla Walla area.

To continue the tour through this historic region, return to Highway 12, and go east toward Waitsburg.

To Waitsburg

Six miles past Isaacs Avenue, the road bisects the small town of Dixie. Soon after leaving Dixie, the highway begins a gradual climb over the divide and into the valley of the Touchet River (pronounced locally as TOO-she).

28

As the highway approaches Waitsburg, note the beautiful views of the Blue Mountains to the south. With the rolling grainfields in the foreground, and the tall mountains in the back, the scenery along this part of the tour is spectacular. Waitsburg is nine miles past Dixie.

Waitsburg is unique. It is the only town in Washington that still operates under its original 1882 territorial charter. Because of that charter, all taxes collected in the city go directly to the city coffers, instead of being dispersed through the state and county.

Waitsburg has an additional claim to fame. The Lewis and Clark Expedition camped on the banks of the Touchet River near the present town the night of May 1, 1806. Highway 12 from Waitsburg to Dayton follows the trail walked by Lewis and Clark in 1806.

The downtown business section is one of the loveliest in the Inland Empire. After a major fire in 1880, a city ordinance required that commercial buildings be built of brick. Several full blocks of beautiful brick structures remain from that rebuilding boom. The entire downtown area is registered as a National Historic District.

The Bruce Memorial Museum at 318 Main Street, is in the residential section of Waitsburg, south of downtown. William Perry and Caroline O'Neal Bruce built this home in 1883. The house was purchased in 1971 by the Waitsburg Historical Society. The house has been completely restored and beautifully furnished by this non-profit group. The Bruce Museum is the best and most attractive historical preservation on this tour. A visit here is well worth the time. Very rare household items, like the isinglass stove and the pump organ in the parlor and the hand-powered vacuum cleaner in the pantry, are displayed. There are no electric lights in the home, which maintains its original appearance. Horse-drawn buggies and sleighs, and old tools and agricultural equipment, are displayed in the carriage house.

The Bruce Museum is open on Friday and Saturday from 1 P.M. until 4 P.M. At other times, the museum can be opened by appointment. Free guided tours are offered by historical society members. The museum is not wheelchair accessible. For more information, contact the Museum at PO Box 277, Waitsburg, WA 99361, (509) 337-6582.

Lewis And Clark Trail State Park

Returning to the tour, continue on Highway 12, eastbound. Four miles from Waitsburg, the tour passes Lewis and Clark Trail State Park. The park provides a large grassy picnic area, complete with drinking water and restrooms. Most of the thirty-seven-acre park is adjacent to the Touchet River. Thirty campsites are located along a loop road on the left side of the highway.

The campsites were constructed by prisoners from the Washington State Penitentiary at Walla Walla. The campsites are separated by thick vegetation for privacy. This campground is the only state park in Washington to provide unpaved grassy campsites exclusively. The loop road through the campground is paved, but each campsite is green. During the summer, an evening campfire program highlighting some aspect of the Lewis and Clark period is offered at no charge. A mile hiking trail and three-quarters of a mile interpretive nature trail are available at the park. Campsites cost seven dollars per night. For more information, contact Lewis and Clark Trail State Park, Route 1, Box 90, Dayton, WA 99328, (509) 337-6457.

To continue the tour, go east on Highway 12 toward Dayton.

Dayton

Dayton is five miles past the state park. Visitors should begin a tour of Dayton at the depot, which is the oldest railroad depot in Washington. It was built in 1881 and donated in 1974 to the Dayton Historical Depot Society. The depot is at the corner of Second and Commercial Streets. To visit the depot, turn left (north) at the only stoplight in Dayton, at the intersection of Second and Main Streets. Main is Highway 12 through the middle of town. The depot is one block north of Main. The stationmaster's quarters upstairs, and the public areas downstairs, have been beautifully restored. A balcony on three sides of the building provides a great view of the town and the surrounding hillsides.

The depot is open for guided tours from 1 P.M. to 4 P.M., Tuesday through Saturday. The depot is not wheelchair accessible. The tour lasts approximately one-half hour and costs one dollar per person.

A free Dayton Visitor Information Guide is available at the depot. It contains a self-guided tour of Dayton's historic homes. More than seventy homes are listed in the guidebook, with a map and background information on each building. Dayton is filled with historic buildings. Eighty-three homes, the depot, three churches and the courthouse, are listed on the National Register of Historic Places. More than three-hundred buildings in the town are more than one-hundred years old. The depot is also the headquarters for the Dayton Chamber of Commerce. The historical society and the Chamber can be reached at PO Box 22, Dayton, WA 99328, (509) 382-4825.

The Columbia County Courthouse, at 341 East Main, one block east of the depot, will soon be renovated and restored. A modern facade will be removed, and the old cupola will be returned to the roof. The work should be completed by the end of 1990, at a total cost of 1.3 million dollars. Much of the courthouse interior requires no restoration. A lovely wooden staircase and high-ceilinged hallways and offices remain in the building. The courthouse was built in 1887, and remains the oldest in the state still used by county government. Visitors can tour the courthouse free, from 8:30 A.M. until 4:30 P.M. weekdays. It is not currently wheelchair accessible, but will be after the renovation.

Perhaps the most unusual business in Dayton is the Patit Creek Restaurant. It is the only three-star restaurant in Eastern Washington, and is consistently rated the "Best French Restaurant" in regional readership polls. Bruce and Heather Hebert opened the Patit Creek eleven years ago. Most of their clientele is from Walla Walla, Spokane, or the Tri-Cities. Only eight tables are available, so reservations are suggested year round, and usually required during the summer. It is open Tuesday through Saturday for lunch and dinner. The address is 725 East Dayton Avenue, Dayton, WA 99328, (509) 382-2625. This ends this tour through the cradle of Inland Empire history. From Dayton, Highway 12 continues east toward Lewiston, Idaho.

The Broughton Dynasty

Dayton's wealthiest family, the Broughtons, have played an important part of the history of the upper Touchet River valley. Charles Julius Broughton, known locally as C. J., arrived in 1872. He left his native Maryland at age 17 to work for his uncle, Charles Fitzland Buck, a freight hauler on the Mullan Road from Walla Walla to Missoula. Broughton earned $40 per month as a cook for the packers. After several seasons on the trail, he operated Buck and Cave's store in Forest City, near Superior, Montana.

In 1878, he travelled to Walla Walla, on the first leg of a trip back to Maryland to visit his family. While in Walla Walla, he met Sid Schwabacher, who hired him as a clerk at McDonald and Schwabacher's general store in Dayton. Broughton abandoned his vacation plans and moved to Dayton.

Two years later, he married a local girl, Ina McCleary. On their wedding night, they moved to the house at 303 E Washington, where they lived the rest of their lives and raised their nine children.

By 1900, Broughton had saved enough to buy out both McDonald and Schwabacher. He then sold the business, but kept the building, and began a successful career as an investor. By 1909, Broughton was wealthy enough to start his own bank, the Broughton National Bank. The family sold the bank in 1958 and it is now the Dayton branch of Seafirst Bank.

C. J. died in 1921, leaving management of the family empire to his eldest son, C. J., Jr. In 1946, his brother, James, became co-manager of the family empire. When the brothers died in 1978 and 1979, their sons, Charles Julius III (known as Chad) and William took over.

"William is running it now; I retired in 1984, though I still work as a consultant on occasion," Chad Broughton explained. "It is a family partnership now, owned by twenty-one cousins."

Chad and Darlene Broughton

The family holdings are immense. In addition to owning much of Dayton's commercial real estate, the Broughtons own twelve-thousand acres of farmland and seventeen-thousand acres of pastureland. The entire operation is managed through the Broughton Land Company, at 200 E. Main. The office is open to visitors. Several old photographs line the walls, including pictures of Chad's father and grandfather. C. J.'s original general store was located across the street from the office.

The Broughton dynasty is continuing. Chad and his wife Darlene have a son, Charles Julius Broughton IV, and he has a son, Charles Julius Broughton V.

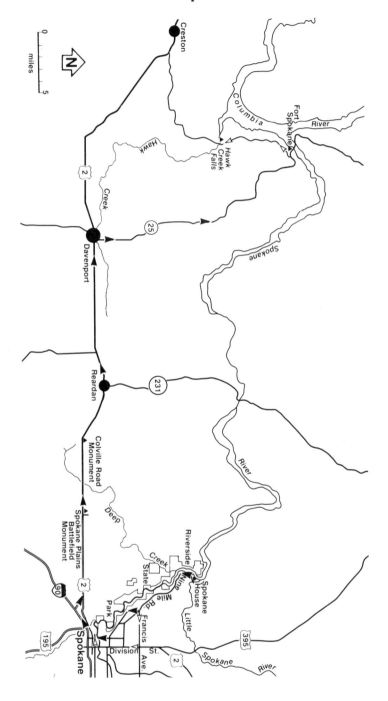

Chapter 4

SPOKANE OLD AND NEW

(68 miles)

Time: A minimum of 1 1/2 hours by automobile.

Services: Restrooms and drinking water are available in Riverside State Park and at Fort Spokane. All services are available in Spokane, Reardan and Davenport.

Bicycles: This tour is well-suited for bicycles. The entire route is paved and most of the roads have wide shoulders. Leisurely bicycling paths and paved roadways fill Riverside State Park, on the first section of the tour. Highway 2 from Spokane to Davenport contains many wide-shouldered sections and is quite level and lovely. The portion from Davenport to Fort Spokane is beautiful and only lightly travelled. Several steep grades are located on this last section of the tour.

Wheelchairs: Unless otherwise indicated, all of the places described in this chapter are wheelchair accessible.

Spokane has grown considerably since fur trappers established the Spokane House trading post in 1810. On this tour, visitors trace the history of the Spokane area and enjoy the comforts and conveniences of the biggest city in the Inland Empire.

The tour begins at Spokane House and ends at Fort Spokane. Along the way, it passes Reardan and Davenport.

The Cowles Media Empire

In 1890, William Hutchinson Cowles went west to seek his fortune. He came to the boisterous frontier town of Spokane as the business manager of the *Spokesman*, one of the local newspapers. Four years later, he bought out the competition, and became the publisher of the *Spokesman-Review*, which is the foundation of his family's financial empire.

Cowles (pronounced coals) was the son of Alfred Cowles, a stockholder and secretary-treasurer of the *Chicago Tribune*. William was educated in French boarding schools and graduated from Yale. Though he came from a life of wealth, he suffered his share of adversity. In 1877, at the age of eleven, he fell from a moving freight train and lost his left leg below the knee. With an artificial leg and plenty of gumption, he was later able to ice skate and ride horses and bicycles.

After working as a police reporter on his father's paper, he went to Spokane and joined the staff at the *Spokesman*. The paper was two months old and losing five-thousand dollars monthly. With money from his family, Cowles kept the paper afloat, and then in 1893, bought the competing *Review*. The first issue of the *Spokane Review*, with W. H. Cowles listed as the publisher, appeared on February 20, 1893. After buying out his three partners the next year, Cowles renamed it the *Spokesman-Review*. At only twenty-eight years of age, Cowles announced in the first issue of the *Spokesman-Review* that he would control both the editorial direction and the business management of the newspaper.

In 1896, he married Harriet Bowen Cheney, the daughter of a Connecticut mill owner. Cowles consolidated his media empire in 1897 by buying the other Spokane newspaper, the *Daily Chronicle*, which served as an afternoon daily in tandem with the morning *Spokesman-Review*.

W.H. Cowles

Cowles dreamed of turning over the papers to his sons, William and Cheney. After William and Cheney graduated from Yale in 1924 and 1930, they began selling advertisements for the newspapers. William H. Cowles became general manager in 1935, as part of a plan to put William in charge of the business functions and Cheney in charge of the editorial direction. Before that plan could be implemented, World War II intervened and Cheney became a US Army major. He was killed in an airplane crash near Mobile, Alabama in 1943. The family established the Cheney Cowles Museum in his memory.

W. H. Cowles died of heart failure in 1946. Although he held the title of publisher, much of the decision-making had passed to William. Today, the publisher of the *Spokesman-Review* is William H. Cowles, III, the grandson of the man who started the dynasty a century ago.

Riverside State Park

Riverside State Park is a 7,655 acre haven for boaters, hikers and campers. It is a long, irregularly-shaped park ten miles northeast of the city on Highway 291.

The Spokane House Interpretive Center is in the north end of the park, at the confluence of the Spokane and the Little Spokane Rivers. The site was chosen in 1810 by fur traders representing the North West Company of Canada. It was the first white settlement in present Washington state. The Hudson's Bay Company closed Spokane House in 1826, moving their operations to Fort Colville near Kettle Falls, Washington. The buildings were stripped of all useful items and gradually disappeared.

The site of the Spokane House was rediscovered after World War II by archeologists. The outlines of the original buildings have been marked in the field adjacent to the interpretive center. The interpretive center contains exhibits of the tools and building materials discovered by the researchers, as well as displays explaining the history of the region. The building is open Wednesday through Sunday from 10 A.M. to 6 P.M. during the summer. Contact Spokane House Interpretive Center, Riverside State Park, Highway 291, Spokane, WA 98205, (509) 456-3964.

To begin the tour, leave the Interpretive Center and turn right onto Nine Mile Road (Highway 291). One-half mile later, the road forks near Nine Mile Dam. Turn right at the fork and drive along the river. Four miles later, the road enters Spokane and becomes a four-lane highway.

One-half mile past the Gun Club Road intersection, turn right onto Assembly Street. One mile later, this street becomes Northwest Boulevard. This route enters Spokane through a residential district along the bluffs above the Spokane River valley. Several small scenic overlooks on the right side of Northwest Boulevard offer vantage points above the valley. Northwest Boulevard deadends at Monroe Street, about nine miles south of Spokane House. Turn right on Monroe and continue ahead one mile to Sprague Avenue.

Spokane Visitor's Center

A good place to begin exploring Spokane is at the Visitor's Center, in the beautiful old Chronicle Building at Sprague and Monroe. The staff at the Visitor's Center can supply information about where to eat, sleep or shop, what events are available during your visit, and what points of interest are located nearby. Several walls in the office are filled with local and regional brochures and maps. A free brochure is available that details a twenty-seven-mile self-guided drive that brings visitors to all city landmarks. The center is open daily. The Visitor's Center can be contacted at West 926 Sprague, Spokane, WA 99204, (509) 747-3230.

While at the center, note the beauty of the Chronicle Building. The lobby is lined with lovely marble and wood. Windows in the lobby offer a view of the newspaper press room. The presses run virtually around the clock printing both local newspapers.

Adjacent to the Chronicle Building is the Spokesman-Review Tower. These two buildings are the heart of the Cowles Publishing Company empire. Tours of the newspaper publishing facility begin on the main floor of the Spokesman-Review Tower. Adrienne Brundage leads free, thirty-minute tours of the facility, from the printing shop to the editorial offices, every Thursday, all day. Reservations are required; phone (509) 459-5068.

Interstate 90 crosses Spokane at the southern edge of the downtown area. To continue this tour, follow Monroe Street south for one-half mile to the I-90 West on-ramp. Continue west on the freeway for two miles to Exit 277.

Highway 2

At Exit 277, go west on Highway 2. The highway passes Spokane International Airport and Fairchild Air Force Base. Nine miles past Exit 277, in the middle of open flat farming country, is a remarkable pyramid-shaped monument on the right. At Dover Road, turn right, and turn left immediately to the monument which is visible from the highway. The fifteen-foot-tall pyramid marks the site of the Battle of Spokane Plains. In 1858, Col. George Wright defeated the combined forces of the Coeur d'Alene, Palouse, and Spokane tribes near this spot, opening the farmland to settlement. The monument, which is one of the most beautifully designed in the region, stands now in a dirt parking lot with no tourist facilities.

Continue west on Highway 2. Six miles later, the highway passes a second monument on the right. This simple roadside marker commemorates the old Colville-Walla Walla military road which crossed Highway 2 here. Five miles later, Highway 2 enters Reardan. Reardan is another slowly dying town filled with empty buildings and vacant homes. The highway bisects the town, and the tour continues west toward Davenport.

Three miles past Reardan, Highway 2 climbs gradually into an area of rolling hills planted to grains. This area is much like the Palouse farmland to the south and east (see Chapter 1 for a description of the Palouse hills). To geologists the area is known as a broad loess upland; to farmers, it is known as good wheat-growing land.

Davenport

Davenport is twelve miles west of Reardan. This prosperous-looking community is the seat of Lincoln County, and the center of a wealthy wheat-growing region.

Highway 2 becomes Morgan Street as it bisects the town. One-half mile ahead, turn left at Sixth Street and continue one block ahead to Park Street. This is a good place to begin a walking tour of Davenport. A small city park at this intersection provides a shady picnic area, drinking water, restrooms and a swimming pool.

The Lincoln County Museum and Information Center is across the street from the park. The historical society built the museum in 1972 to display household items and old photogaphs from the area. Many of the exhibits, like the stereoptican and the model planetarium, are available for handling and close inspection. The most unusual and gruesome display is the death mask of Harry Tracy, a renowned outlaw who killed himself to avoid capture in 1902. Tracy's death mask shows his skull shattered by the suicide bullet. The museum is open daily during the summer, and by appointment in the winter. Admission is free. The building is not wheelchair accessible. Contact the museum at PO Box 896, Davenport, WA 99122, (509) 725-6711.

Lightning Nuggets, an interesting local business, invites visitors to stop and tour their manufacturing facilities. Lightning Nuggets are balls of wax and sawdust used to start fires in stoves or fireplaces. They are still made in Davenport by the family of the man who invented them. Marshall Thompson and his wife, Sharon, made the nuggets as a hobby, then turned it into a profitable business. Now the fire-starters are sold throughout North America, in catalogs and in outdoor supply stores. The Thompsons' two sons, Jay and Jeff, now run the family business. The Thompsons offer free tours on weekdays but ask that visitors call ahead for directions and reservations. Contact the Thompsons at (509) 725-6211.

Channeled Scablands

To continue the tour, return to the east end of Davenport on Highway 2 (Morgan Street), then turn north onto Highway 25. The tour passes through loess soil farmland for six miles until the highway dips into the first of a series of channeled scabland valleys. In these valleys, the fertile soil was eroded, exposing the underlying black rock. Sagebrush is virtually the only plant that grows on the valley floors.

The loess soil was washed from those valleys by the largest series of floods in the world. During the last Ice Age, about ten-thousand years ago, a dam was created by glaciers in the narrow valley of the Clark Fork River, near the present Idaho-Montana border. A huge lake, known to geologists as Glacial Lake Missoula, was created behind the dam. Periodically, the dam burst and the water released, scouring the flatlands and gouging deep channels into the soil. These catastrophic floods created the channeled scablands — a series of wide parallel valleys eroded down to bare rock. This tour crosses several of those channels, part of the Davenport-Creston Scabland Tract.

About twelve miles from Davenport, to the left, note the canyons dropping to the Columbia River below. The tour continues toward Fort Spokane. Four miles from the Porcupine Bay campground entrance, note the Christ Lutheran Church on the left. This is one of

The Hansens of Reardan

The two-story grey house at the corner of Highway 12 and Aspen Street, in the middle of Reardan, is Bernie Hansen's home. The house and the Hansen family have both been in the midst of things in Reardan for a century. Bernie's grandparents homesteaded west of Spokane in 1886. To support themselves, they took in boarders. One man who boarded with them was the railroad design engineer, Charles Fairfax Reardan, for whom the village was named.

Bernie's father, John Hansen, built the home in 1903. It is one of the oldest buildings in town, and the lasting beauty of the structure is a testimony to his craftsmanship. John was also a lumberman, cement culvert maker, mechanic, and hardware store owner. His business, originally Hansen's Paint Store, was housed in the now-empty cement block building across Highway 12 from the Hansen home. John built that building in 1919 from cement blocks he cast himself.

Bernie Hansen with his player piano and music box.

Bernie Hansen was born in the home in 1908. Music is one of the fondest memories of his childhood. "My father played the accordian; he was the only musician in the area at the time," Bernie said. "He played for dances all around here, including many dances in this living room." A player piano and hand-cranked music box remain in the Hansen home from those days. His home is filled with other mementos and antiques from Reardan's past. The home is noted for its beautiful interior woodwork. The doors, windows, framing and wainscotting were all created by John Hansen. Bernie has opened the home for public tours during local Centennial celebrations. When his health is better, he may do so again.

Bernie has lived in Reardan, and in his house, for virtually all of his life. Though many of those years were spent caring for invalid relatives, his memories of Reardan's past are warm ones. "It was always a farming community, but larger then. The Highway was just a gravel road to Spokane then. Reardan has always been a nice friendly place to live." Bernie is a lifelong bachelor, so the future of the Hansen home is in question.

the earliest churches in the area, built in the 1890s. The church is at the head of Bockemuehl Canyon, which the highway follows down to the Columbia River. The tour now enters a Ponderosa Pine forest. Approximately five miles past the church, stop at the wide overlook site on the right. The beautiful Columbia and Spokane River valleys are visible from this site. Fort Spokane is visible at the confluence of the two rivers.

The tour continues north on Highway 25. One-half mile past the viewpoint, Highway 25 crosses the Creston Road. A small store and gas station are located at this intersection. This tour ends one-half mile ahead on Highway 25 at Fort Spokane. Visitors can take the sidetrip to Hawk Creek Falls by turning at this junction.

Optional Sidetrip To Hawk Creek Falls

From the intersection of the Creston Road and Highway 25, turn south on the Creston Road. This two-lane, paved road climbs to the bluffs overlooking the Columbia and parallels the river for seven miles to Hawk Creek. Hawk Creek is at the Big Bend of the Columbia, where the river makes a sharp right turn and heads west toward the Cascade Mountains.

Turn off the paved road to the right, following the signs toward Hawk Creek Campground. The campground is at the end of a half-mile-long gravel road. The campground offers drinking water, pit toilets, a boat ramp, and a dock.

Hawk Creek Waterfall is about fifty yards from the eastern edge of the camping area and can be reached by following an obvious trail. A wide rock bowl has been cut by the creek, and the falls drop about fifty feet from the top of the rock cliff into the bowl. Flocks of swallows nest on the cliffs above the pool. In the afternoon, the sun fills the bowl for delightful swimming. The pool is over ten feet deep. For a refreshing stop on a hot day, Hawk Creek Falls has few equals.

To return to the tour, retrace the roadway north to Highway 25, then turn left toward Fort Spokane.

Fort Spokane

The US Army established Fort Spokane in 1880 to protect settlers in the upper Columbia River Valley. By 1892, forty-five buildings stood at the site, and more than three hundred soldiers and their dependents lived here. The presence of the troops may have been an adequate deterrent, because the soldiers never fired a hostile shot. During the Spanish-American War, the army moved to Fort George Wright in Spokane. The fort buildings became the headquarters of the Colville Indian Agency. In 1929 the site was abandoned and many of the buildings were destroyed. In 1960, the fort was transferred to the National Park Service and the four remaining buidings were restored.

The visitor center is in the old guardhouse near the center of the fort grounds. The fort and the visitor center are open daily at no charge. A free self-guided tour leads visitors through the entire site. A ten-minute slide show is offered at no charge in one of the guardhouse cell rooms. Exhibits of Army equipment are displayed in the other rooms of the guardhouse and the other restored buildings.

Fort Spokane is part of the National Park Service's Coulee Dam National Recreation Area. The adjacent campground offers sixty-two non-hookup campsites for six dollars per day. A wide sandy beach, boat dock and launch ramp, and a grassy picnic area on the river are available nearby. Contact Fort Spokane at HCR 11, Box 51, Davenport, WA 99122, (509) 725-2715.

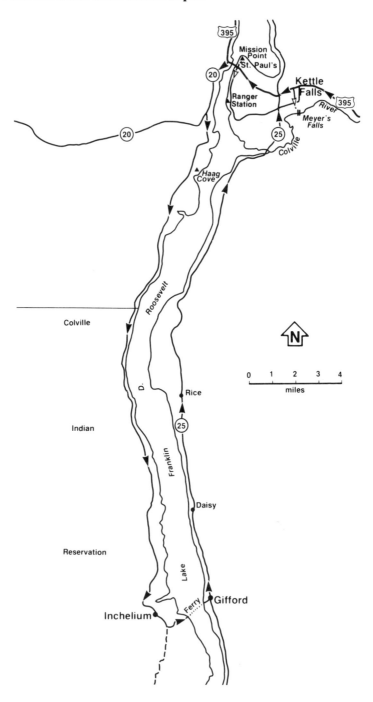

Chapter 5

FINDING THE FREE FERRY

(35 miles)

Time: A minimum of one hour by automobile.

Services: All services are available in Kettle Falls and Inchelium. Drinking water and restrooms are available at the Kettle Falls Ranger Station, and at both docks of the Inchelium-Gifford Ferry.

Bicycles: This is an excellent biking route. The road is paved and mostly flat. The portion of the tour that follows Highways 395 and 20 offers wide paved shoulders. Cyclists can use the sidewalk on the south side of the bridge to cross Lake Roosevelt. The Inchelium Road is very narrow and has unpaved shoulders, but the traffic is light.

Wheelchairs: Unless otherwise indicated, all of the places described in this chapter are wheelchair accessible.

   This tour begins in Kettle Falls, eighty miles north of Spokane on Highway 395. Kettle Falls was named for the series of waterfalls on the Columbia River. Salmon migrating upstream to spawning beds swam and jumped up the cascades, exposing themselves to netting and spearing. Because of this excellent fishing opportunity, the area was a fishing, camping, and trading place for members of the surrounding tribes for more than nine-thousand years.

In 1811, David Thompson, an explorer and mapmaker for the North West Fur Company, visited the area. In 1825, Hudson's Bay Company built a trading post and stockade by the portage route around the falls. The post was named Fort Colvile, for Andrew Colvile, a company director. More than three-hundred acres of land adjacent to the fort was cultivated, and the produce was shipped to settlements along the Columbia River and even to Alaska. The post closed in 1871.

The town of Kettle Falls was incorporated in 1892, and became a major agricultural and transport center. In 1941, the town, Fort Colvile, and the falls themselves were flooded by Lake Franklin D. Roosevelt. The lake was created by Grand Coulee Dam, more than one-hundred miles downstream. Before the water rose, the town of Kettle Falls was moved five miles to its present location, the site of the settlement of Meyer's Falls, which was renamed Kettle Falls.

This Columbia River valley location is beautiful, and the surrounding rocky hills are covered with Ponderosa Pines. Lake Roosevelt is Washington's largest lake, 151 miles long, offering splendid fishing and boating opportunities. The summer climate is ideal, dry and sunny. Virtually all of the lake's shoreline is unpopulated.

Kettle Falls

An unusual billboard appears at the entrances to town: "Welcome to Kettle Falls, Home of 1224 Friendly People...and one grouch." The community grouch is selected annually by election. Each vote costs twenty-five cents, and the money raised is used to purchase holiday gifts and food for local needy families. Don't expect to be accosted by any grouches, it's all in fun, and the locals are friendly.

Information about Kettle Falls is available at a self-service information center on Highway 395, at the eastern edge of town. The center, which is not wheelchair accessible, is open twenty-four hours a day, seven days a week. Volunteers occasionally staff the building. It is filled with free brochures and announcements of upcoming events. For more information, contact the Kettle Falls Chamber of Commerce at PO Box 119, Kettle Falls, WA 99141.

Those with unanswered questions should visit the Double H Motel, adjacent to the information center. J. D. and Ann Anderson, the motel owners, volunteered to place the center on their property and to respond to all the requests for more information. The address of the Double H is 205 E Third Street, Kettle Falls, WA 99141, (509) 738-6514.

Happy Dell City Park is located on Third Street (Highway 395) at the west end of town, opposite the big Boise Cascade lumber mill. This park offers restrooms, drinking water, a covered picnic area, a children's play area, and tennis courts, all available at no charge.

The tour continues to the original site of Meyer's Falls. Just east of Happy Dell Park, turn south onto Juniper Street, and continue ahead for one mile. Drive past the Kettle Falls High School, then watch for the sign on the right: "Meyer's Falls Hydroelectric Project, WWP." Turn right at the sign, down the gravel road about fifty yards to a parking lot.

Meyer's Falls is a series of twenty-foot cascades along the Colville River. Foot paths wind from the parking lot through the lovely river valley to fishing holes and picnicking rocks. In 1903, a water-powered flour mill was built there, and the foundations are still visible in the canyon below the parking lot. A twenty-four-foot-tall dam was built there in 1915, and is still in use. A self-guided nature trail follows the perimeter of the eleven acre reservoir, and a small fishing dock extends into that reservoir. Drinking water and restrooms are not available here, but the picnicking and exploring potential is unexcelled.

Return to Kettle Falls and turn left onto Highway 395 (Third Street) to continue the tour.

Optional Sidetrip To Mission Point

About three miles west of Kettle Falls, before the Columbia River bridge, turn right onto the gravel road marked St. Paul's Mission Road. For anyone interested in local history or just a chance to visit some of the area's most beautiful lakeside vistas, this sidetrip is a must.

The gravel road follows the old portage route around the Kettle Falls. Boats could not navigate the falls, so boats and cargo were carried around the falls. About one-half mile from the highway, the road ends at St. Paul's Mission. The original post-and-beam structure, made of huge, hand-hewn timbers, was finished in 1847 by Jesuit missionaries. The mission was abandoned in the 1880s, and the building eventually collapsed. In 1939, this replica of the mission building was built on the bluff above the river.

The mission site is open during daylight hours. The building itself is unlocked, and on a hot day, the thick walls keep the interior cool and refreshing. A half-mile-long self-guided trail around Mission Point offers plenty of lovely lakeside viewpoints. The trail is wheelchair accessible, but the mission building is not. Signs along the trail identify the locations of Fort Colvile and Kettle Falls, which are now under water. In the spring, when the water level is lowered, the foundations of the fort and several riverside towns are exposed.

As you return to the highway, notice the empty building on the left side of the Mission Road. This is the future home of the Kettle Falls Historical Center. A non-profit group is raising the money to finish the interior of the building and display artifacts of local tribal, fort and mission history. The opening date for the museum has not been announced. For more information, contact the Kettle Falls Historical Center at PO Box KFHC, Kettle Falls, WA 99141.

Return to Highway 395 and turn right toward Roosevelt Lake.

On The Road To The NRA

Continue down Highway 395 for fifty yards past St. Paul's Mission Road, then turn left onto the road to Kettle Falls Ranger Station. The intersection is well-signed.

The lakeshore around Lake Roosevelt was designated Coulee Dam National Recreation Area in 1946. It is administered by the National Park Service. The office is two miles from the highway and provides free brochures on the recreational opportunities of the area and a small display of historic artifacts. A seventy-six-unit campground is adjacent to the ranger station, and thirteen other campgrounds are located nearby. The office is open weekdays and intermittently at other times. For more information, contact the Kettle Falls NRA office, Rt. 1, Box 537, Kettle Falls, WA 99141, (509) 738-6266.

A marina, convenience store, dockside gasoline, a free boat launch ramp and dock are located near the ranger station. The marina rents canoes, paddleboats, skiboats, and fifty-foot houseboats. From May to November, the marina is open from 8 A.M. to 8 P.M. For more information, contact Lake Roosevelt Resorts and Marinas, PO Box 340, Kettle Falls WA 99141, (509) 738-6121 or (800) 635-7585.

While visiting the marina, include a stop at the net pens, located on the small dock at the end of the parking lot. Four twenty-foot-square floating pens along the dock hold thousands of rainbow trout. The trout are raised by a non-profit group for release into Lake Roosevelt. The dock and net pens are open for inspection at any time, at no charge. For twenty-five cents, visitors can buy a bag of fish food at a dispensing machine at the end of the dock. When the food is thrown into the pens, the water explodes in a frenzy of flashing tails and fins. There is no better show for a quarter.

To return to the tour, retrace the route north toward Highway 395. Halfway between the ranger station and the highway, on the left, is a Boise Cascade mill, which is open for free guided tours. Visitors can call ahead to reserve a time, or just show up and try to arrange a tour. The company requires that visitors wear hard-toed shoes, be prepared for walking, and bring no one younger than teenagers. This tour is not wheelchair accessible. Weekdays are best, but some weekend tours are possible. For more information, contact Boise Cascade, PO Box 310, Kettle Falls, WA 99141, (509) 738-6421.

Highway 395 is one mile past the Boise Cascade mill. At the highway, turn left. The bridge over Lake Roosevelt is just past the turn.

Fun for Fruit Fans

Wayne McMorris is a big man with a huge smile. He and his wife, Corene, own a cherry, peach, apricot, pear, apple, and nectarine orchard on the bluffs above Lake Roosevelt — an area he calls "the very best fruit-growing region in the Western United States." "I've been around fruit all over the West, and if I could pick any place to grow fruit, it would be here," Wayne said. "The soil is perfect and so's the climate — plus we need only limited irrigation which makes the fruit very sweet. This area grows the best fruit in the West, and our customers say so, too."

Fruit-lovers from Canada, Idaho, Montana, and Washington make annual pilgrimmages to Kettle Falls to buy from fifteen orchardists who sell fruit directly to the public. Those fifteen are members of a loosely-knit organization called the Upper Lake Roosevelt Orchard Directory. The group exists only to publicize the local harvest and to encourage travelers to stop and buy fruit from their orchards.

In 1988, the group printed a brochure, the "Driving and Information Guide to the Many Family Owned Orchards near Kettle Falls, Washington." Because of the quality of the fruit and the brochure, local fruit sales expanded rapidly. Local production doubled in recent years, and virtually all the fruit from Kettle Falls orchards is now sold directly to residents and visitors. "We're doing so well that we don't need to do anything else but that one flyer," Wayne said with an especially big smile.

Though he is reluctant to admit it, Wayne can take much of the credit for the success of the grower's organization and the directory. With fellow orchardist Joanie Matter, Wayne developed the concept, then invited other local growers to the group's first meeting. They all came, and everyone contributed some money to print the brochure.

Wayne and Corene McMorris.

Visitors can either pick from the trees, or buy fruit already picked. For the best flavor, the fruit offered for sale will be tree-ripe and just-picked. The growers also provide guided tours of their orchards.

The free directory is available in brochure racks throughout the Inland Empire. It is available by mail from Peachcrest Fruit Basket, South 855 Peachcrest Road, Kettle Falls, WA 99141, (509) 738-6305.

Across the River and Back Again

From his seat at the control panel thirty feet above the deck of the river ferry *Columbia Princess*, Mike Seyler has a magnificent view of the wide blue lake and the forested mountains that cascade to the edge of Lake Roosevelt. As Seyler remarks, "it's a beautiful place for a boat ride."

Seyler is the senior pilot on the ferry route between Inchelium and Gifford which crosses the lake every fifteen minutes during his eight-hour shift. He joined the crew in 1977 and became a pilot in 1978.

"That winter of '78-'79 was the coldest in years," he recalled. "The river froze six inches thick and we only had the tug and barge then. We had to ram the barge over and over into the ice to break a trail. We almost had to shut down for the winter. But the night after we decided to shut the ferry down, it thawed and all the ice melted."

Seyler began piloting on the *USS Kohler*, a tugboat attached to a barge. The barge was docked by sliding it against the shore, and the cars were unloaded by driving off a lowered ramp. The pilot steered by turning a large wheel, which tired even the strongest captains. Traveling in fog, without radar, the pilot was forced to rely on a compass. In 1982, Seyler was glad to see the *Columbia Princess*, their new ferryboat.

The *Princess* was built at Everett, Washington, in 1981, and cruised upriver to Inchelium the next year. It is a 110-foot-long, ninety-five-ton, double-ended ferry with four engines and four pivoting propellers. It is a modern boat, complete with radar and electronic controls. The ship fits snugly into cement docks at both ends of the route.

"It is a lot different than the old cable ferry my father used to run here," Seyler noted. Mike's father, Thomas Seyler, was a ferry pilot at the Inchelium-Gifford crossing in the 1920s

54

and 1930s, before the Grand Coulee Dam raised the water level and submerged the old cable ferry.

Mike Seyler was born nearby, at Twin Lakes, on the Colville Indian Reservation. He is a Lake Indian, one of the half-dozen bands within the Confederated Colville Tribes. About half the ferry crew are tribal members. Roy Weatherman, the man who has the ferry contract with the Bureau of Indian Affairs, is an Indian as well.

As a youth, Mike admits that he got in a lot of trouble fighting. At age nineteen, he moved to Oregon to become an amateur, and then a professional, boxer. "I won the Oregon Golden Gloves title at age twenty, and then a few years later, by the mid-1970s, became Oregon's professional middleweight champion," he said. "But I got tired of the big cities, the airplanes, the travelling, and after nine years without getting hurt, I decided it was time to get out. I came home. Now you can't get me to leave. When my vacation time comes, I don't go anywhere—I've got everything I want right here."

On the left, immediately past the bridge, is a small pullout. Those who want a great view up and down the lake can park at the turnout and walk back across the bridge on a narrow sidewalk on the south side of the bridge.

The Road To Inchelium

About fifty yards beyond the bridge, turn west (left) on Highway 20 toward Republic. Four miles later, turn left onto the paved road to Inchelium. This intersection is well-marked. For the next twenty-five miles, the road parallels the western shore of the lake. This area is virtually unpopulated, with only scattered ranches giving evidence of human habitation. Excellent views of the lake and the forested hillsides are found all along this route.

About two miles from Highway 20, the tour passes the entrance to the Haag Cove Campground. This camping area offers a lovely beach, pit toilets, drinking water, tables, grills, and a boat ramp.

Seven miles past Haag Cove, enter the Colville Indian Reservation. This 1.3 million acre reservation was established in 1872. The road through the reservation runs along the shoreline, and waterfowl are visible on the marshes at the water's edge. Roadside turnouts are scattered along this road for photography, birdwatching, or picnicking.

Twenty miles past Haag Cove, the road to the local Bureau of Indian Affairs office intersects the Inchelium Road. The BIA officials can answer questions about camping on reservation land. The tribal authorities control the lakeshore on the reservation, and their camping rules are more relaxed than the regulations set by the National Park Service for the rest of the lakeshore. The BIA office, which is not wheelchair accessible, is open weekdays from 7:30 A.M. to 4 P.M. For further information, contact the Bureau of Indian Affairs, Inchelium, WA 99138, (509) 722-4161.

Two miles past the BIA entrance road, the tour enters the small town of Inchelium. Continue through town to the ferry dock, three miles south of Inchelium.

The Inchelium-Gifford Ferry

The *Columbia Princess* ferryboat is owned by the Bureau of Indian Affairs. As part of the US Government's treaty obligation to the Colville Tribe, the ferry is maintained to replace a river crossing which was submerged beneath the lake. The ferry is free to all, and there are no restrictions on the size of motor homes or trailers. The ferry operates every day, from 6:30 A.M. to 9:45 P.M. The ride across the three-quarters-of-a-mile-wide lake takes five to ten minutes. The ferry leaves Inchelium on the hour and the half-hour. It leaves Gifford at fifteen and forty-five minutes after the hour. Restrooms and drinking water are available at both docks.

Riding the ferry is a beautiful way to enjoy the lake. Waterskiers, testing their skill, often ride in the ferry's wake. Waterfowl are commonly seen. After leaving the ferry, this tour ends at Highway 25, about fifty yards from the dock. Two National Park Service campgrounds, Gifford and Cloverleaf, are located to the left (north), within two miles of the dock.

Though this tour covered only thirty-five miles, it is one of the most beautiful trips in the Inland Empire. With a free ferry ride as part of the bargain, this could be the best tour in this book.

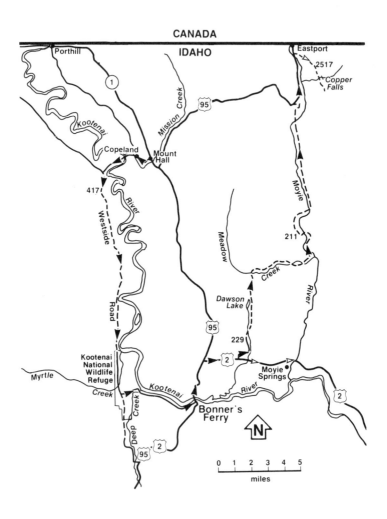

To Canada, the long way.

Chapter 6

TO CANADA, THE LONG WAY

(54 miles)

Time: A minimum of two hours by automobile.

Services: All services are available at Bonners Ferry, the midpoint of this tour. Gasoline and groceries are available at Mount Hall, at the beginning of the tour, and at Eastport, at the end. Restrooms and drinking water also are available at the Kootenai National Wildlife Refuge, the Meadow Creek Campground, and the US border inspection station at Eastport.

Bicycles: This tour is poorly-suited for most bicycles, because most of the route follows gravel roads. However, since these roads have few steep grades and many beautiful vistas, they are well-suited for experienced mountain bike riders.

The portion of the tour through the Kootenai National Wildlife Refuge and along the river into Bonners Ferry is a good bicycling road. The roadway there is paved and flat, but it is narrow in parts, so bicyclists must be careful.

Wheelchairs: All places described in this chapter are wheelchair accessible, unless otherwise indicated.

Boundary County, Idaho's northernmost county, seems to be either horizontal or vertical. The mountains are steep and rugged, while the valleys are flat. This contrast produces scenes of great beauty, with picture-postcard vistas of beautiful farms and towering peaks.

This county is also a travelers' delight because it is virtually unpopulated. The county has a population of about 4,500; about half of whom live in Bonners Ferry. The people are outnumbered by deer, elk, moose, bear, and waterfowl.

This fifty-four mile journey through Boundary County avoids the primary paved highways for most of its length. The gravelled roads are slower, but the views are superb, and the chance for solitude and observation are much improved. This tour begins at the tiny village of Mount Hall, on Idaho Highway 1, just north of the intersection of Highway 1 and Highway 95. Mount Hall is about seventeen miles north of Bonners Ferry and ten miles south of the Canadian border.

On The Road To Westside

Mount Hall is a tiny town with only one business, the Mission Creek Store. From the store, go about one-quarter mile north, then turn left onto County Road 45. The intersection is marked with a sign pointing toward the Copeland Bridge and Westside Road.

This paved county road crosses a flat bench above the river, winds between forestland and small farms, then descends to the riverside floodplain. Continue across the Copeland Bridge over the Kootenai River. Ahead are the rugged and rocky peaks of the Selkirk Mountains. Behind are the Purcells, not quite so pointed, more weathered, but still tall and impressive. The valley between the two mountain ranges is the Purcell Trench, a deep channel excavated by glaciers, then filled with lakes made of melting glacial ice. When the glaciers disappeared about ten-thousand years ago, evidence of the passing Ice Age remained in the form of lakes, including Lake Coeur d'Alene and Lake Pend Orielle, and the long flat channel now occupied by Highway 95. This tour begins in the Purcell Trench.

The Copeland Bridge is two miles from Highway 1. Drive slowly over the bridge to see the beauty of the Kootenai River as it winds northward into Canada, its banks lined with huge cottonwood trees.

Two miles past the Copeland Bridge, turn left onto Westside Road. The junction is well marked. This road parallels the Kootenai River, sometimes passing through the forests along the base of the mountains, and sometimes through the valley floor. When the road clears the trees, the views of the green valley floor, the trees, and the mountains are magnificent.

About one-quarter of a mile from the junction of County Road 45 and Westside Road, watch for the sign on the left marking the entrance to Elk Mountain Farms, a subsidiary of Anheuser-Busch, the world's largest brewer. The corporation came to Bonners Ferry to grow and process hops, an ingredient vital in beer-making. For two years, the company has been planting hops and building the huge trellises that support the vines. By 1991, the thousand-acre operation is expected to produce about two million pounds of hops annually.

Anheuser-Busch chose this area because it is the same latitude and climate as the regions in Germany that grow the Hallertauer hops, a variety which is prized in brewing. That variety had been grown in the area successfully by local farmers. When Anheuser-Busch arrived, the company purchased all the local operations and is now the sole grower and processor of hops in the region.

For a view of the hops fields, stop at the pullout on the left, below the Elk Mountain Farms sign. At the entrance to the farm, three miles ahead, the processing plant and the apartment building for the farm's migrant workers is visible in the middle of the fields. At the farm entrance, the main road seems to curve left into the farm. That's because most of the traffic on Westside goes to this farm. Follow Westside Road straight ahead at this junction, across a small bridge. After crossing the bridge, the road is narrower and unpaved, but is passable for all vehicles.

Drive slowly along Westside Road and watch for wildlife. Deer and moose cross the roadway and waterfowl visit the ponds scattered throughout the valley. Plenty of pullouts dot this part of the tour and the road is usually traffic-free.

Several cattle ranches are located along Westside Road. The road is often paved for a few hundred yards in front of the houses and barns to control road dust. The big barns in the area, built with unusual arched or curved roofs, were designed to store hay.

Kootenai National Wildlife Refuge

About fifteen miles from the Copeland Bridge, the tour enters the Kootenai National Wildlife Refuge. The road is paved from this point. The office is on the left, two miles beyond the entrance to the refuge just past the bridge over Myrtle Creek. The office is open Monday through Friday from 8 A.M. to 4:30 P.M. Drinking water and restrooms are available at the office. The refuge is open at no charge the year round. No camping is allowed. Free brochures are offered at the office. A listing of bird arrival dates is also posted there. From the office, a self-guided one-way-only automobile tour winds four miles through the refuge and rejoins Westside Road at the southern end of the refuge. For more information, contact the Kootenai National Wildlife Refuge at HCR 60, Box 283, Bonners Ferry, ID 83805, (208) 267-3888.

This tour follows Westside Road south. At the fork one-half mile south of the refuge office, follow the main road to the left. Two miles from the refuge office, the tour leaves the refuge and crosses the Deep Creek Bridge. The entrance to the Deep Creek boat launch and picnic area is located on the left, just past the bridge.

Several picnic tables are under the trees along the riverbank. A large parking area, a boat launch ramp and dock, and pit toilets are available, but no drinking water is provided. This is the best local public access point to the Kootenai River.

At this point, the tour follows the road built top of a dike. About one-half mile past the Deep Creek Bridge, note the small glacial "islands", covered with trees and brush in the flat grainfields on the right. These are the tops of small granite hills that survived the grinding of the glaciers that formed the Purcell Trench. Three miles from Deep Creek Bridge, the tour enters Bonners Ferry.

Without a Refuge, Where Would the Birds Go?

The Kootenai National Wildlife Refuge was established in 1965 to reclaim wetlands along the Kootenai River. When the marshes and ponds were drained and diked by farmers, the waterfowl that traditionally used the area were left without a stopover on their annual migrations. To provide a haven for the birds and other wildlife, 2,774 acres were acquired by the US Fish and Wildlife Service. Water from nearby Myrtle Creek is piped into the refuge to maintain a dozen ponds on the refuge. Someone has to make sure the dikes hold water, primarily by battling the beaver and muskrats. The muskrats drill burrows into the banks which cause spills and leaks; the beavers plug culverts and water structures by building dams. The beavers and muskrats are trapped for relocation.

In 1978, Bruce Frazier started working at the refuge as the maintenance specialist. "That means I do anything that's needed to keep things going," he explained. "I repair equipment, mow trails, keep the ponds filled, build nesting boxes, plant feed—anything."

Frazier also plants feed for waterfowl. In the spring, he plants small acreages of barley. In the fall, when the crop matures, he floods the fields, creating a pond full of prime bird feed.

"This is a damn good job; it's my kind of work," Frazier explained. "I work out in the open, and get a chance to see plenty of wildlife. I also feel real good that I'm doing something to help conserve wildlife. Since I've been here, I've seen a lot more elk and moose—their numbers are really growing around here."

Frazier has seen huge flocks of ducks and geese. Thousands of visitors yearly visit the refuge. In the spring, they watch the fowl raise their young; in the summer, they see the wide variety of songbirds; and in the fall, they watch the migrating flocks resting and feeding on their southward migration.

Bonners Ferry

Bonners Ferry was named for Edwin Bonner, who operated a ferryboat here from 1864 to 1875. Most of the travellers were miners headed for the goldfields of British Columbia over the Whitehorse Trail. By the 1880s, the town became a major supplier for the mines to the north. In 1883, steamboat service on the Kootenai River linked the town to Canada. By 1893, the town was named Bonners Ferry.

The Kootenai Tribe of Idaho originally inhabited the Boundary County area. Their history is unique and interesting. At the time of the Hellgate Treaty of 1855, the first treaty between the US Government and the northern tribes, the Kootenais were not represented. As a result, they were not given a reservation and became landless. Although the tribe was totally neglected by the federal government over the next century, the Kootenais retained their cultural traditions.

Anger at the lack of a reservation surfaced on September 20, 1974 when the Kootenais declared war on the US. As a result of this bloodless war, they were given an eighteen-acre reservation three miles northwest of Bonner Ferry. Only about 120 tribal members remain today and about half of them live on the reservation. The tribe is trying to develop jobs and an economic base for its future. Their first project was the forty-eight-room Kootenai River Inn, a luxury resort on the banks of the Kootenai River adjacent to Highway 95/2 in Bonners Ferry. Tribal crafts are sold in a store in the resort's lobby. For more information, contact the Kootenai River Inn, Kootenai River Plaza, Bonners Ferry ID 83805 (208) 267-8511.

North Toward Canada

The tour continues on Highway 95/2. From Bonners Ferry, follow the highway north across the river. The road climbs steeply to a flat bench filled with grainfields and pastureland. On the left, two miles from Bonners Ferry, a historical marker notes the passage of David Thompson, pioneer map maker and fur trader. The North West Company of Canada sent him here in 1808 to explore this region. He arrived three years after Lewis and Clark explored the Columbia River, two hundred miles south of here.

About one-half mile past the historical marker, Highways 95 and 2 divide. Turn right on Highway 2. Two miles from the junction, turn left on Meadow Creek Road, which is also known as Forest Road 229 and County Road 34. The intersection is well marked.

Optional Sidetrip to Moyie River

To view the Moyie (pronounced locally as MOE-yay) River canyon and the Moyie Falls Dam, continue ahead on Highway 2 toward Montana. About four miles ahead, Highway 2 crosses the Moyie River on the second highest bridge in Idaho. The bridge is 1,223 feet long and the bridge deck is 464 feet above the river.

At the far (or east) end of the bridge, turn right to the overlook. The intersection is well signed. The view of the bridge and canyon is worth a stop. A small park near the overlook offers picnic tables, drinking water, and barbeques, but no restrooms.

Those who want a closer look at the canyon should return to the east end of the bridge and park at the pullout on the right at the edge of the highway. A narrow sidewalk across the bridge, provides splendid vantage points from the center of the bridge. The sidewalk is not wheelchair accessible.

To resume the tour, retrace the route, going west to Meadow Creek Road.

Along The Moyie River

Meadow Creek Road is paved for two miles, then turns to gravel, but remains passable for all vehicles. The road winds through a beautiful forest of alder and birch, passing small farms mingled with forestland and Dawson Lake.

Nine miles from the highway intersection, the road crosses railroad tracks, then forks. The right fork is the entrance to the US

Forest Service's Meadow Creek Campground. The campground offers twenty-three free campsites, drinking water, and restrooms. The campground was built at the site of the old town of Meadow Creek, which is now completely gone.

Turn left at the fork onto Forest Road 211. For the next ten miles, the tour parallels the Moyie River, a beautiful and untamed mountain river. In the early summer this river is a favorite of rafters. Dozens of access points and riverside pullouts make viewing the river and its rocky canyon very easy. Forest Road 211 is heavy on the wildlife and very light on the traffic. It is a beautiful nineteen-mile trip.

Road 211 ends at Highway 95. Turn right on Highway 95 and continue north toward Canada.

Optional Sidetrip To Copper Creek Falls

To visit Copper Creek Falls, turn off the highway about three miles north of the intersection of Highway 95 and Forest Road 211. Follow Forest Road 2517 to the right. The intersection is well marked. This is a narrow gravel road which is passable to all vehicles.

Follow Forest Road 2517 for one mile to the entrance of the US Forest Service's Copper Creek Campground. This free campground is located at the edge of the Moyie River. Sixteen campsites, restrooms and drinking water are available there.

Continue past the campground entrance for 1 1/2 miles to the trail to Copper Creek Falls. Stop at the small pullout on the right side of the road. A pit toilet is on the right, and the trail begins on the left or uphill side of the road. The half-mile-long trail is wide and gradual enough for wheelchairs. The trail ends at a fenced overlook site with a great view of the one-hundred-foot-high waterfall. Copper Creek drops in one cascade down a sheer rock face to a small pool. The falls are delicate and lovely.

To continue the tour, go back to Highway 95 and turn right.

Canada

The tour continues north on Highway 95 to the Canadian border. The border is one-half mile north of the intersection with the road to Copper Creek Falls. The small town of Eastport, Idaho, is at the border. The US and Canadian border inspection stations are open twenty-four hours a day. Restrooms and drinking water are available at the US station.

Those continuing on to Canada can buy liquor, tobacco or perfumes at reduced prices at the duty-free store, located at the border. Those products can be purchased without tax, which results in significant savings. There is a catch, however. These items must be sold to Americans who will consume the products while visiting Canada. The products cannot be brought back into the US. For more information, contact the Idaho Store, PO Box 33, Eastport, ID 83826, (208) 267-7326.

Notice the thirty-foot-wide swath through the forest along the U.S.-Canadian boundary. To mark the border, American and Canadian authorities cut down all vegetation on both sides of the line.

WASHINGTON

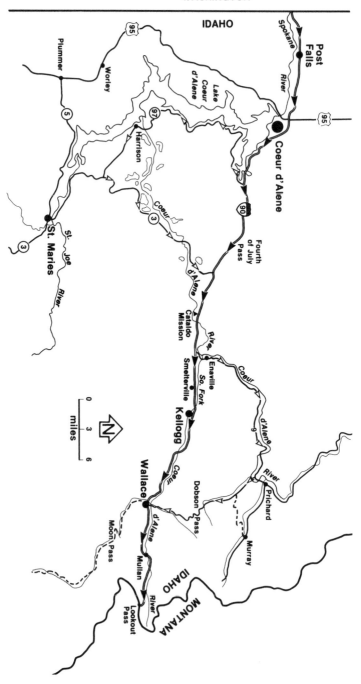

Chapter 7

FREEWAYS CAN BE FUN

(80 miles)

Time: A minimum of about one and one-half hours by automobile.

Bicycles: Traveling on this portion of I-90 is forbidden. Well-marked alternate bike routes, along paved frontage roads, parallel the Interstate for most of the tour. No good alternate routes are available for crossing Fourth of July Pass between Coeur d'Alene and the Silver Valley, and Lookout Pass on the Montana border, so bicyclists must use the freeway shoulder.

However, bicycling this tour is a good idea, as there are several excellent sidetrips worth sampling. Within Coeur d'Alene, lakeside roads and bikeways (from Tubbs Hill to Fort Sherman) are heavily traveled, but offer an enjoyable three-mile journey. Also, there is a fifty-seven-mile paved route, winding and sometimes narrow, from the junction of I-90 and Highway 97 south past Harrison to Highway 3 then back to the junction of Highway 3 and the I-90. This beautiful route follows the eastern shore of Lake Coeur d'Alene, then returns up the valley of the lower Coeur d'Alene River. The third bike sidetrip leaves the I-90 at Exit 43, near Kingston, and follows the upper Coeur d'Alene River past Enaville, looping back over Dobson Pass to I-90 at Wallace. This thirty-nine-mile paved route is narrow and steep over the pass, but very beautiful along the whole distance.

69

Wheelchairs: Unless otherwise indicated, all the places described in this chapter are wheelchair accessible.

Freeways are boring. High-speed highways are designed to get you there, not to enchant you along the route. But this tour follows a different kind of freeway across the Idaho Panhandle.

Beginning at the Washington border, just before Post Falls, and ending at the Montana border, past Wallace, this freeway is fun. The folks who live along the I-90 corridor are doing their best to entice travelers to stay and enjoy the lakes, mountains, and rivers — plus all the resorts, theme parks, and attractions opened in recent years. The area is doing its best to become the "Playland of the Northwest."

A quick drive along this tour requires less than two hours. A see-it-all trip across the Panhandle can easily stretch to a two-week vacation, or more. You can camp, fish, swim, hike or hunt in some of the prettiest backcountry in the West. Then for variety, you can stay in an elegant resort, walk deep into the tunnel of a silver mine, ride America's largest gondola, enjoy gourmet dining at its finest, or dig into the fascinating history of the richest silver-mining region in the world. All of that, and more, is available on this tour.

In Idaho On The Interstate

The tour begins on I-90 at the Idaho-Washington border, about twenty miles east of Spokane. In Idaho, each offramp is numbered with the approximate mileage from the Washington border. This tour identifies the offramps by their exit numbers. The tour follows the Spokane River for the first dozen miles. The river is the outlet for Lake Coeur d'Alene, connecting the 25,000 acre lake with the Columbia River.

One mile into Idaho, on the right, is the new Coeur d'Alene Greyhound Park, the only dog racing track in the Inland Empire. The track was opened in 1988. The greyhounds run daily all year, and the general admission fee is one dollar. Video seminars on the wagering system, plus demonstrations by one of the betting clerks, are available for free before the first race every day. Entry to the dog track is from Exit 2 just ahead. For more information about the greyhound track, write to PO Box 880, Coeur d'Alene, ID 83814 or phone (800) 828-4880 or (208) 773-0545.

Post Falls

Post Falls is the first town on this tour. Frederick Post came to the area in 1871 and negotiated a treaty with Chief Seltice (pronounced sell-TEECE) of the Coeur d'Alene tribe. Post purchased land near a waterfall on the Spokane River for his mill. In 1884, he built a small dam and the first sawmill in the Kootenai County area. By 1891, the town was incorporated. In 1911, the Post Falls Dam was completed, providing electrical power to the area and maintaining Lake Coeur d'Alene at a constant elevation for navigation and recreation purposes.

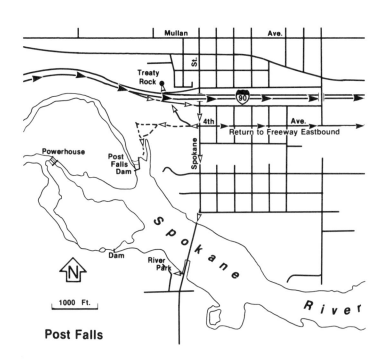

Post Falls

The name Coeur d'Alene (French for "heart of an awl") was originally given to the local Indians by French trappers because of their shrewd bargaining abilities and independent nature. The name is now shared by the city, the lake, the river, and the tribe. (It is pronounced locally as cordle-AIN.)

Treaty Rock, where Post and Seltice recorded their pact, is near the Interstate. Turn off at Exit 5. At the bottom of the exit ramp, turn right onto Spokane Street, then turn right at the first intersection, Fourth Avenue. Park by the fenced substation directly ahead, about fifty yards from the intersection of Fourth Avenue and Spokane Street. Treaty Rock is two-hundred yards down the path on the right. This wide, paved path goes under the freeway, then enters a wooded area that is pretty enough for a picnic, but with the traffic above, a little too noisy for relaxation. Behind the fenced area are the marks left by Seltice and Post on the side of a boulder. Unfortunately, graffiti vandals armed with blue spray paint have visited the rock, but the red designs and marks made a century ago are still visible.

To continue the tour, walk back to your vehicle. Those who want a closeup view of Post Falls Dam should continue driving around the fenced substation to the left. Drive one-half mile on this dirt road, circling around the Louisiana-Pacific lumber mill. At the locked gate directly ahead, follow the road to the left through the trees. A small parking lot and a chain link fence are straight ahead. The dam is just past the fence. Park there and walk up one of the trails to the right. The trails are not suitable for wheelchairs.

As you walk up the hill and toward the left, the narrow canyon below the dam is ahead. Post Falls Dam is visible there by the parking lot, a tiny plug for a huge lake. The flat rocks by the canyon's rim are great for picnics. Drinking water or other facilities are not available at Treaty Rock or Post Falls Dam.

To continue the tour, return to Spokane Street. Turn right (south) onto Spokane Street, and go to the Community Park at the far end of the Spokane River Bridge. Turn right on the first road after the bridge to enter the park. Restrooms, drinking water, a boat launch ramp, a sandy beach, and picnicking space under the trees are available in the park.

The Spokane is a working river, and tugboats still move logs to the Louisiana-Pacific mill on the water. The big resort hotel on the opposite shore is Templin's Resort and Marina. This four and one-half million dollar resort complex, completed in 1986, has 110 rooms and a sixty-slip marina. Most rooms have river views. Templin's address is 414 East First Avenue, Post Falls, ID 83854, (208) 773-1611.

Continue the tour by returning to I-90, then go east.

Coeur D'Alene

Exit 11 is the entrance to the city of Coeur d'Alene and to the lake of the same name. Turn right off the Interstate and continue two miles down Northwest Boulevard to the lakeshore. Just before the lake, the road curves left and becomes Sherman Avenue. The first stoplight past the curve is Second Street. At the stoplight turn right (toward the lake). After the road curves to the left, look for the huge free parking lot on Front Street between Third and Fourth. Park there. That's the best place to begin a visit to Coeur d'Alene.

The town has welcomed tourists to its lakefront since the first excursion boats hauled passengers around the lake sixty years ago. The welcome mat is still out today. The best way to enjoy the lakeshore is to use the walking/biking/wheelchairing pathway system along the lake. The pathway connects Coeur d'Alene's five lakefront parks.

Tubbs Hill Nature Preserve and The Lakefront Pathway

Adjoining the parking lot to the south is a forested peninsula known as Tubbs Hill Nature Preserve. Tony Tubbs was a German immigrant who filed a claim to this hill in 1882. He sold the land as homesites, and it was not until 1977 that the last of the 135 acres was repurchased for public use as an undeveloped natural park. A two-mile loop trail skirts the edge of the hill, and several secondary trails crisscross the park. The trails are not designed for wheelchair use.

A brochure, the Tubbs Hill Nature Trail, describing the forestland environment turns the Tubbs Hill loop trail into a self-guided nature walk. It is available for free from local businesses or from the Coeur d'Alene Chamber of Commerce. The Chamber office, which

73

Into the Sixth-Floor Cellar

The chance to tour a fully-stocked wine cellar with a recognized wine professional — at no charge — is one of the more surprising options in Coeur d'Alene. Sam Lange is the wine steward at Beverly's, the seventh-floor restaurant in the Coeur d'Alene Resort. As wine steward, Lange is responsible for purchasing and storing the wine for the restaurant. He also spends most of his evenings there, helping diners choose an appropriate bottle for their table.

"I try to open every bottle, to present the wine at the table and talk to our guests," said Lange, thirty-three. His personal involvement also includes tours of the hotel's cellar — a state-of-the-art facility of which Lange is very proud.

"This is not some romantic underground atmosphere," Lange explained. "This is a high-tech facility, built with long-term cellaring requirements in mind." The cellar (on the sixth floor, directly beneath the restaurant) is well insulated, vibration free, with constant temperature and humidity.

The wine tour at the resort includes a quick trip through the restaurant, famed for its lovely lakeside views and the bright copper accents of its interior, and a stop at the Cruvinet. The Cruvinet is a wine dispenser that enables the restaurant to offer glasses of the finest wines to those who do not wish to purchase a full bottle. But the highlight is a trip down the stairs to the sixth-floor cellar. "It is quiet and pretty in the cellar — all very beautifully done in tile with plenty of wine bins," he added. "I love it there; it's a wonderful place for lovers of wine."

Beverly's is the ideal place to choose from an amazing variety of wines. Because of the wide selection and premium choices offered on their wine list, Beverly's was one of only seventy-four restaurants worldwide selected to receive the "Best Award of Excellence" by *Wine Spectator* magazine.

"We now offer more than 525 items on our wine list and retain over 15,000 bottles in our cellar," Lange said. "Of course, we are always expanding, going on buying trips to California, visiting estate sales, looking for wines not locally available."

Among his finer vintages are several rare Red Bordeaux, dating back to 1928 and a Chateau Latour, on sale for $3,500. The list also includes a selection of California reds, California Chardonnays and the best Pacific Northwest wines.

Lange is generally available to lead tours of the cellar and the restaurant from 3:30 P.M. until 5:30 P.M. Tuesday through Saturday. Reservations are required for the tour and recommended for the restaurant. Phone (800) 826-2390 from the Continental US or (800) 841-5868 from Idaho.

is not wheelchair accessible, is one block from the parking lot at 140 South Second Street. Their mailing address is PO Box 850 Coeur d'Alene, ID 83814, (208) 664-3194. The Chamber can answer questions about things to do in the area and festivities planned during your stay.

The Tubbs Hill Nature Trail provides beautiful views of the town's lakefront and the forested hillsides along the lakeshore. Adjacent to Tubb's Hill, to the west, are the free public boat launch ramp and docks. The Fun Fleet, four big passenger boats that offer sightseeing tours, departs from those docks daily in the summer. Information about Fun Fleet cruises is available from the Coeur d'Alene Resort, the eighteen-story hotel adjacent to the docks. The resort's mailing address is: On the Lake, Coeur d'Alene, ID 83814. Phone (800) 826-2390 from the Continental US or (800) 841-5868 from Idaho.

When the resort opened in 1986, it included a park and a boardwalk, both open to the public at no charge. The park is the five-acre plaza with the clocktower between the resort and Sherman Avenue. The boardwalk is the world's largest floating boardwalk, built around the marina adjacent to the eighteen-story lakefront tower. The boardwalk is ten feet wide and almost three-quarters of a mile long, and comes equipped with plenty of benches and even some planter boxes filled with trees and flowers. The walkway is the best place to watch the sailboats on the lake. The boardwalk is wheelchair accessible from the eastern end, near the Fun Fleet dock. The full length of the boardwalk is not wheelchair accessible due to a stairway.

The pathway system that unites the Tubbs Hill Preserve, the boardwalk, and the Plaza continues to westward to fifteen-acre Coeur d'Alene City Park. The park features a sandy swimming beach and a grassy picnic space under a canopy of big trees. Drinking water, restrooms, and restaurants are available in the park.

Museum of North Idaho

Adjacent to the park, at 115 Northwest Boulevard, is the Museum of North Idaho, the best place to learn about the tribes, steamships, logging, mining, and the rest of the history of the area. A one dollar donation is requested at the door. The museum's mailing address is PO Box 812, Coeur d'Alene, ID 83814, (208) 664-3448.

Return to I-90 to continue the tour.

For seven miles past Coeur d'Alene, lake access points are scattered along the route. Along the highway, stairs leading to small docks have been built for free public use. Extra wide shoulders allow anglers and boaters plenty of room to pull off the highway to test the lakewater. At mile 17, a historic marker documents the use of steam-

More to See in Coeur d'Alene

There's more to Coeur d'Alene than the attractions along the lakeshore. Several more interesting stops beckon travelers.

The US Forest Service Nursery has grown more than 400 million trees for planting in forests throughout the region. Guided tours are offered weekdays between 8 A.M. and 3 P.M. Call ahead, if possible, to (208) 765-7375. During some periods in the spring and fall, the nursery personnel are too busy packaging trees to lead tours. The address is 3600 Nursery Road, Coeur d'Alene, ID 83814.

The Sunshine Mining Company operates the Sunshine Silver Mine near Kellogg and their office in Coeur d'Alene is the only place where anyone can be assured of buying silver from Idaho mines priced at the daily fluctuating "spot price." The spot market is the price on the international commodity markets. Delivery of the silver is immediate for those who pay with cash. Those who pay with a check can expect delivery by mail in a month. The office is open weekdays from 8 A.M. to 4 P.M.. The address is 7405 North Government Way, Coeur d'Alene ID 83814, (208) 772-9592 or toll-free (800) 322-1944. Mining artifacts and silver bars are displayed in the lobby.

T. W. Fisher's beer micro-brewery offers guided tours of the brewery, complete with beer tasting daily at no charge. Contact T. W. Fisher's, 204 North Second Street, Coeur d'Alene, ID 83814, (208) 664-2739.

ships on the lake, beginning with a US Army supply ship in 1880 and the first commercial steamers in 1884.

Optional Trip To The Lower Coeur D'Alene River

The sidetrip to the lower Coeur d'Alene River valley, along Highways 97 and 3, is a lovely fifty-mile journey perfect for those who like beautiful lakes and a chance to fish or birdwatch. At Exit 22, take State Highway 97 south, to the right. This highway winds along the beautiful eastern shore of Lake Coeur d'Alene, past the mouth of the Coeur d'Alene River toward St. Maries. Before St. Maries, turn left onto State Highway 3, which follows the Coeur d'Alene River north and back to the Interstate. To continue the tour, go East on I-90.

Fish Inn

At Exit 22, travelers will find one of Idaho's most shapely taverns, the Fish Inn. Turn left at the end of the offramp, then left at the T intersection fifty yards ahead. The Fish Inn is one hundred yards ahead on the left.

Yes, the Fish Inn looks like a fish, a big-mouthed bass about ninety feet long and twelve feet wide. The open mouth is the door, and the tail points toward the Interstate. The Inn was built in 1932 as a restaurant specializing in spaghetti and hamburgers. Now it is a tavern that sells food, too. The atmosphere is now pure honky-tonk, with plenty of country tunes on the juke box, a large outdoor deck area, and signed dollar bills plastered over the bar. The Fish Inn is a good contrast to the elegance of Coeur d'Alene's lakeshore. The address is Fish Inn, 10000 East Yellowstone, Wolf Lodge Bay, Coeur d'Alene, ID 83814, (208) 765-8536.

To continue the tour, go east on I-90.

Fourth Of July Pass

The freeway soon starts winding and climbing, crossing Fourth of July Pass. The pass got the name because Capt. John Mullan's Army roadbuilding crew camped at the summit on July 4, 1861. The crew was constructing the Mullan Road from Fort Walla Walla to Fort Benton.

78

Camping and fishing opportunities abound in the mountains. After descending the east slope and leaving the forest, the tour enters the valley of the Coeur d'Alene River. The valley here is broad and lush, surrounded by timbered hillsides. The Jesuits chose this as the center of their mission to the Coeur d'Alene Tribe.

Coeur D'Alene Mission

Old Mission State Park was created to preserve Idaho's oldest standing building, the Jesuit's Mission of the Sacred Heart. The park is adjacent to the Interstate. Leave the freeway at Exit 39 and turn right. The park entrance is one-half mile south and is clearly marked.

The Jesuits built their first mission in 1842 in the valley of the St. Joe River about forty miles south of here. Repeated flooding forced them to find a better site. In 1846, they selected a grassy knoll near the Coeur d'Alene River as the place for their mission.

The church was built by 1853 and is now fully restored. In 1961, the mission was designated as a National Historic Landmark; in 1975, it became an Idaho State Park. The church is the oldest standing building in Idaho.

A grassy picnic area is next to the parking lot near the Visitors Center. A free, ten-minute slide show is offered on request at the center. The center also contains restrooms, drinking water, a gift shop, a soda pop dispenser, and exhibits from the church's history.

The mission church itself is a remarkable structure, built of huge hand-hewn timbers and planks connected with wooden pegs. The walls were made using the wattle and daub system. Horizontal sticks were first placed between the upright beams, then meadow grasses were folded over the sticks. Mud was placed onto the grasses, and the result was something like an adobe wall. Inside the church, portions of the wattle and daub wall have been exposed in rooms off the sanctuary. Religious services are held there only on special holidays.

From the mission, a half-mile-long, self-guided trail circles down to the parking lot. Several old cherry and apple trees line the trail. A free brochure details the historical and natural points of interest along the trail. A second brochure describes the placement of buildings around the original mission complex.

The eighteen acre park is open from March until November. There is a two-dollar per vehicle entry fee. For more information, contact the park at PO Box 135, Cataldo, ID 83810, (208) 682-3814.

Retrace the road back to the Interstate to resume the tour.

The Silver Valley

The Silver Valley begins near Exit 43, where the South Fork of the Coeur d'Alene River parallels the Interstate. The Silver Valley, known also as the Coeur d'Alene Mining District, is the world's richest silver mining area. There are over ninety mines in the district, including the largest underground mine in the US (the Bunker Hill Mine, with more than 150 miles of tunnels) and the deepest mine in the US (the Star-Morning Mine, which is more than 7,900 feet deep). Miners have taken more that a billion ounces of silver, eight million tons of lead, three million tons of zinc, and significant amounts of other metals from this part of Idaho since 1884.

The metals are found in veins within the dark, layered "Belt Supergroup" rocks that are now exposed on hillsides and roadcuts throughout the area. The Belt rocks are more than a billion years old. After the rocks were formed, mineral-bearing waters were forced from below into cracks in the rock. After the water disappeared, the minerals, including the valuable metals, were left in the veins in the rock. The miners dig tunnels into the veins to remove the mineral-bearing rocks.

Precious metals were first discovered by A. J. Prichard, who found gold near Osburn in 1878. Prichard later discovered gold near Murray, in 1881, sparking a gold rush. The gold boom soon died, but prospectors drawn to the region discovered lead and silver deposits.

Kellogg

After passing Exit 43, the Interstate enters an area of incredible devastation. The freeway passes through acres of waste rock and

Optional Dobson Pass Sidetrip

An optional thirty-nine-mile sightseeing loop begins at Exit 43. From this interchange, Forest Road 9 winds northward along the Coeur d'Alene River, beginning a paved loop route that returns to I-90 at Wallace. This loop route is beautiful, and well suited for those who wish to avoid towns and traffic, but fuel is not available on this sidetrip.

To take this loop route, go north from the Interstate at Exit 43. The Enaville Resort is 1 1/2 miles north of that exit. It is a huge log slab building built in 1880 and rebuilt after a fire in 1918. Now it is a family restaurant and tavern, but originally it was a bar and brothel. The red light bulb remains in the cow skull above the front entrance. That red bulb was lit whenever the brothel was open for business.

The restaurant is furnished in an eclectic western decor, complete with mining artifacts and chairs made from elk antlers. Enaville is a full-menu restaurant now, and the specialty is "Rocky Mountain Oysters," sliced and grilled bull testicles. The building is not wheelchair accessible. For more information, contact Enaville at HC 01, Box 250, Kingston, ID 83839, (208) 682-3543.

To continue on the loop sidetrip, head north from the Enaville Resort. The road is lovely as it parallels the Coeur d'Alene River for the first half of the journey. Several small lodges and taverns are scattered along the route. The second half of the journey, over Dobson Pass, is forested. Near the top of the pass, note the beautiful views of the steep canyons adjacent to the road. This sidetrip ends where Forest Road 9 meets I-90. Go east on I-90 to continue the tour.

smelter slag from the mines. Toxic fumes from the smeltering and milling operation on the right killed the vegetation on the hillsides.

The site of the Bunker Hill Mine was discovered by Noah Kellogg in 1885. The 715-foot-high smokestack at the smelter and the

610 foot stack at the zinc plant were added in 1978 to meet local anti-pollution requirements. In 1981, the Bunker Hill Mine was closed due to falling prices for metals and rising production costs. More than 2,100 jobs were lost. Unemployment in the area rose above fifty percent and many residents left the valley.

There is hope now in this scene of destruction. Federally-mandated cleanup operations have begun, and the worst of the environmentally destructive practices have stopped. Trees and bushes are returning to the empty hillsides. In 1988, the Bunker Hill Mine reopened on a smaller scale, under tighter environmental controls.

Another sign of life is the billboard just before Exit 49 which reads, "Willkommen zu Kellogg." The old mining city is being remodeled and renovated, putting on a Bavarian village face. Instead of giving up and moving away when the mines closed, residents decided to strengthen the economic base of their community by encouraging tourism. They want travelers to find their city interesting and inviting enough for a stop, and maybe a closer look.

The Bavarianization campaign has achieved some success. The town is cleaner, and many businesses have added Bavarian-style facades to their buildings. To make the campaign truly successful, they are awaiting the completion of their gondola.

The gondola project, after a decade of debate, is due to be finished by mid-summer 1990. When complete, it will be North America's largest gondola. The eight-passenger cars will be lifted by cable from the valley floor to the top of Kellogg Peak. The seventeen minute ride will carry visitors more than three miles and four thousand feet in elevation to the ski lodge at the peak. The gondola ride will offer panoramic views of the valley and the surrounding mountains. The lift will operate year round, hauling skiers in the winter and hikers in the warmer months. It is expected to cost thirteen million dollars. To many residents, the gondola is the salvation of their local economy.

To visit Kellogg, take Exit 49. Turn left at the end of the offramp, go under the Interstate, then turn right on Cameron Avenue, fifty yards ahead. At the northeast corner of that intersection, look for the big white dome-shaped building at the corner of the parking lot for the

Shoshone Medical Center. That's the office of the Kellogg Chamber
of Commerce and a good place to start a tour of the city. Brochures
and information about Kellogg and the Silver Valley are available at
the Chamber office. Some ore carts and mineworker transport cars are
displayed there. The address is 712 W. Cameron Avenue, Kellogg, ID
83837, (208) 784-0821.

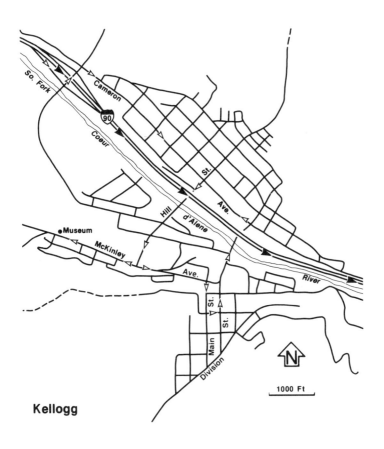

Kellogg

Continue east on Cameron, toward Kellogg. Five blocks later,
turn right at the four-way stop sign, onto Hill Street. Continue under
the freeway to the center of town. On both sides of the street, look for

the unusual metal sculptures along the route. The sulptures, the work of local artist David Dose, are welded from castoff parts of automobiles, stoves, and washing machines. The artworks are remarkably lifelike renderings of Noah Kellogg, dragons, airplanes and locomotives. Four of the large sculptures are on public display along Hill Street just after the freeway underpass.

Continue south on Hill Street for about one-half mile until the road ends at McKinley Street. Turn right on McKinley and drive a half mile ahead to the Shoshone County Mining and Smelting Museum. The museum is in the big white house built for Stanly A. Easton, chief executive of the Bunker Hill Mine Company. Later, it housed visiting dignitaries. The museum is free, though donations are accepted. The museum is open from early June till late September, in the afternoons, from Tuesday through Sunday. The building is not wheelchair accessible. The address is 820 McKinley Avenue, Kellogg, ID 83837, (208) 786-4141.

On the museum grounds are displays of ore carts and other mining equipment. Inside, the focus is on mining history and an extensive mineral collection. Displays from the homes of mining executives and prospectors are also offered.

The Bunker Hill Mine property begins adjacent to the museum, and McKinley Avenue goes right through the mine property. To view the demolished buildings and vacant lots of the Bunker Hill site, drive west along McKinley through the smelter and milling area till you can't stand the devastation any longer. Then reverse course, head east on McKinley, retracing your path toward downtown Kellogg.

To continue the tour, turn north on Hill Street, go back to the Interstate and then take the I-90 to the east.

Wallace

At mile 61, I-90 stops and traffic is directed to the old highway through Wallace. The stoplight on the highway in Wallace is the only stoplight on I-90, from Seattle to Boston. But not for long. For more than a decade, federal authorities have tried to build a freeway past the town. The freeway is scheduled to open in 1991. When I-90 is relocated, the city center will be much quieter. Wallace is a personable and lively community, well worth a visit. It's a town with a strong committment to its roots and an amazing hundred-year history.

Optional Mining Memorial Sidetrip

Those interested in more local mining history can take a short sidetrip to the Memorial for the Sunshine Miners. To begin the sidetrip, follow Hill Street under the Interstate. Do not turn onto the on-ramp. At the four-way stop at Cameron Avenue, turn right. The road continues east parallel to the Interstate. This route is marked Business I-90.

Half a mile later, on the left, note a local landmark, the Miner's Hat. This building, constructed in the shape of a miner's hat, was a tavern. It is now the Miner's Hat Realty. The adjacent hillsides offer an opportunity for a close inspection of the Belt Supergroup rocks with veins of ore.

Four miles from the Miner's Hat, the Memorial to the Sunshine Miners is on the left side of the road. This monument commemorates the death of ninety-one miners in the 1972 Sunshine Mine fire. The men perished in the worst mining disaster in recent history. The memorial is an impressive twelve-foot-tall sculpture of a miner with his drill raised, surrounded by plaques listing the names of the dead. A light burns constantly from his mining helmet.

At the memorial, turn right, from Business I-90 onto Big Creek Road, go under the Interstate and then left onto the freeway onramp headed east. The tour continues along the Interstate to Wallace.

The townsite was just another wide spot on the Mullan Road until Col. W.R. Wallace arrived in 1884, bought the land and built a cabin. His wife Lucy came in 1885, and became the first postmistress. Mines were opened throughout the area, and a narrow-gauge railroad came up the valley in 1886. Wallace became a hub for mining activity in the east end of the Silver Valley. **During boom times, it was one of the richest towns in America.**

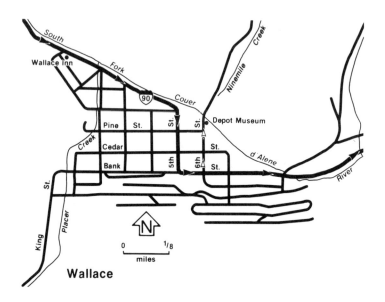

Wallace

Wallace is the best destination on this tour for travelers who enjoy visiting towns smaller than Coeur d'Alene. Kellogg is building the gondola and adding the Bavarian theme, hoping to become the tourism center of the Silver Valley. But Kellogg has one handicap that Wallace managed to avoid. The destruction that accompanied the last century of mining is an inescapable part of the scenery at Kellogg. In Wallace, however, the untidy remains of the mining process are hidden in side canyons, so the town is surrounded by beautiful forests.

The valley is very narrow, and the town is only a half-dozen blocks wide, giving Wallace an Alpine feeling. The surrounding mountains are beautiful, and the town is filled with lovely turn-of-the-century brick and wood buildings.

The best way to begin a visit to Wallace is by walking around town. A free walking tour brochure is available at many businesses and at both museums. As the guidebook explains, Wallace is filled with so many old buildings in such good condition that the entire town is listed on the National Register of Historic Places. During the town's boom times, nationally-known architects designed numerous ornate structures which are identified in the guidebook. Visitors will find many interesting shops, a community art gallery, a melodrama theatre, and jewelry stores in the downtown area. There's plenty to see.

One must-see place in Wallace is the old train depot, now the Northern Pacific Depot Railroad Museum. The depot was one of very few built in the US in the Canadian chateau style. Its distinctive round turret has become Wallace's symbol. The depot dates from 1901, and the twelve-inch-wide bricks that form the walls of the first floor were imported from China, probably as ships' ballast. The depot was slated for demolition to make way for I-90, but the community would not let that happen. In 1986, it was moved across the tracks to its present location, a grassy park by the river.

The railroad museum is filled with a wonderful collection of well-displayed historic railroad equipment. The upper floor contains a huge illuminated sign showing the Northern Pacific Railroad routes from Chicago to the West Coast. The sign originally hung in the Spokane station. The depot museum is on the corner of Sixth and Pine Streets. An entrance fee of one dollar for adults and fifty cents for children is charged. The museum is open daily during the warm weather months. For more information, contact the museum at PO Box 469, Wallace, ID 83873, (208) 752-0111.

Across Sixth Street from the depot is the Jameson hotel and restaurant built in 1908. It is fully restored and houses a lovely restaurant and tavern. The Jameson is at 304 Sixth Street, Wallace, ID 83873, (208) 556-1554.

The other museum in town is the Wallace District Mining Museum. It houses the best historic mining collection in the valley. Especially interesting are their three-dimensional models of the shafts and tunnels of two nearby mines. They also offer a slide show and plenty of other exhibits. The museum's address is 509 Bank Street, Wallace, ID 83873, (208) 753-7151. Admission is one dollar for adults and fifty cents for children, but admission is free if you take a tour of the silver mine first and present your tour ticket at the museum.

Sierra Silver Mine Tour

The mine tour starts from the ticket office adjacent to the mining museum. The tour is about one hour long. A seventeen-passenger tram — a replica of a San Francisco cable car — picks up passengers in front of the mining museum every twenty minutes daily, from 9 A.M. until 4 P.M., from mid-May through September. Tickets for the one-hour tour cost $4.50 for adults and $3.50 for children. Children younger than four are not allowed in the mine. Neither the mine nor the tram ride are wheelchair accessible. More information about the tour is available from Sierra Silver Mine Tour Company, PO Box 712, Wallace, ID 83873, (208) 752-5151.

Though the tour is one of the most expensive activities suggested in this guidebook, it is worth every penny. Tram driver Ed Eckel is entertaining and knowledgeable (he spent thirty-three years as a geologist). The open tram is a great way to see the town, and the mine is the best chance most of us will ever have to walk deep into the earth.

The tram ride takes visitors to the Sierra Silver Mine, two miles north of Wallace on Nine Mile Creek Road. The Sierra Silver Mine opened in 1907, and after it closed, was reopened as this tour destination. At the entrance to the tunnel, the guide offers a short talk about the history of hard rock mining in the area, then everyone puts on a hardhat to enter the mine. For visitors taller than six feet, the hat is a necessity, since some parts of the tunnel have six foot ceilings.

Past the wooden entranceway, the tunnel was driven through solid rock and there are no internal supports. The tunnel tour extends almost a quarter-mile straight into the earth. Veins of ore are clearly visible, and the equipment used to blast and haul the rock are on display. The guides actually operate some of the machinery used in that mine. The machinery is very loud, which is why young children are excluded from the mine. But for everyone else, it's a journey into the past and into the earth that's worth a try.

More To See In Wallace

After the tram returns to Wallace, those who want to see jewelry made from local silver should walk just east of the tram stop to Silver Dynamics. This is the only jewelry store in Wallace which manufactures commercial jewelry solely from Idaho silver. The address is 515 Bank Street, Wallace, ID 83873, (208) 753-7541. The store is not wheelchair accessible. Free tours of their manufacturing area, at the rear of the store, are offered daily on request.

One of the most surprising options offered in Wallace is at the new sixty-three-room Wallace Inn on the west edge of town. Gourmet meals are served with elegance at the Molly B Restaurant by a knowledgeable and personable staff. Locating such fine dining in Wallace is astonishing, and that makes the Molly B a restaurant worth noting, for travelers who want a memorable meal to cap off a visit to the Silver Valley.

Executive Chef William Basham is the reason for the artistry in food at the Molly B. After twenty years of dining experience, he designed the space and the menu to suit his interest in gourmet food and elegant presentation. The Molly B is small; there are only seven tables in one rather simple room. The focus is on the food, with no flashy decor or fabulous views to detract from the dining itself. His goal is to create the finest fine dining establishment between Seattle and Denver; those who drive hours to eat there agree. Contact the Molly B at the Wallace Inn, PO Box 867, Wallace, ID 83873, (208) 752-1252.

From Wallace, roads lead in all directions to forestland and creekside, and to mining areas amazing in their history. Two sidetrips, one to the forest and one to the mines, are offered here.

Sidetrip Through The Forest

For those who want to sample the raging creeks and the steep-sided mountains, a pleasant thirty-five-mile sidetrip goes from Wallace to Avery, a small logging town on the St. Joe River. From the highway in Wallace, turn right onto Second Street. Second Street is the one-way street immediately east of the Wallace Inn and adjacent to the Placer Creek channel. This cement channel was built to contain the raging waters of Placer Creek. Continue on Second Street one-quarter mile to High Street, and turn right. After crossing Placer Creek, turn left at King Street. Follow King Street up the hill.

At the edge of town, the road rises steeply, and the mountains close in on the narrow valley. Placer Creek is freed from its cement channel there and flows swiftly over small waterfalls and through rocky pools. It's a lovely little valley.

Three-quarters of a mile from town, adjacent to the roadway on the left, the US Forest Service erected two monuments to the people who fought the big fires of 1910, and those who perished in the flames. In August of 1910, more than three million acres of timber and part of Wallace were consumed by that huge fire. Edward C. Pulaski led forty-five firefighters that summer. Near the monument site, the crew was trapped by the flames. Pulaski led them to safety in an abandoned mine shaft. One of the monuments was placed in his honor. (Pulaski is also known as the inventor of the "pulaski" - a fire-fighting tool used by foresters.)

Past the monument, the road follows Placer Creek to Moon Pass and then into the St. Joe River valley. The road becomes a well-maintained gravel roadway soon after the monument. Along the route there are some great views of both drainages. In addition, this road provides access into some wonderful backcountry for camping, hiking, hunting and fishing. Consult the US Forest Service for information about facilities along this route. The road to Avery is not a loop route; it's thirty-five winding miles one way. If you don't want to go all the way to Avery, you can turn around at many points along the road and return to Wallace.

Sidetrip To The Mines

The mining sidetrip begins at downtown Wallace and ends at Murray, twenty-five miles away. Though the part of the journey over Dobson Pass is steep and narrow, the entire route is paved and passable to all vehicles. Begin on Sixth Street in front of the depot museum. Follow Sixth Street north, across the railroad tracks and up Nine Mile Creek.

On the right, just past an old warehouse one-quarter mile from town, look up the hillside to the very unusual home. Jerry McKinnon lives in that house. Even though his home is in town, he is a hermit. He will talk with only a handful of people. He was born and raised in Wallace; his relatives bring supplies to him. McKinnon built the two spaceships attached to the home and painted the huge cartoon characters on the outside walls. Sometimes McKinnon ventures onto the lot below the house where he practices lassoing a post. He will not talk to visitors, but does not mind being watched.

The road passes the Sierra Silver Mine (the mine tour destination) on the left. Just past that mine, the old Wallace Miner's Cemetery fills a hillside to the left. The cemetery is well-maintained and contains many century-old graves.

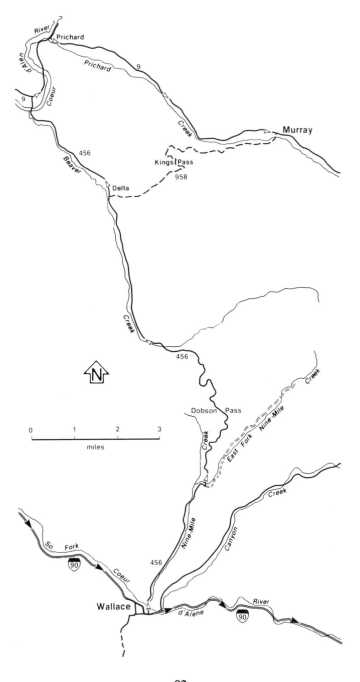

Three miles from Wallace, the Day Rock Mine appears on the left. This mine is fenced to keep visitors away. Just past the Day Rock Mine the paved road forks off to the right. Follow the pavement.

One hundred yards past the first fork, the road forks again. The sidetrip follows the paved route curving left. The route winds uphill following Nine Mile Creek. The road climbs steeply to the summit six miles from Wallace. Beautiful views of the surrounding countryside are provided on both sides of the divide.

Two miles past the summit, the road flattens again as it follows Beaver Creek. The creek is well-named, as lots of beaver dams and lodges fill the creekbed. This is cattle country, with small hayfields and ranches filling the valley. This is also open range country. Watch for cattle on the roadway.

Sixteen miles from Wallace, the Beaver Creek Road ends at the Forest Road 9, along the Coeur d'Alene River. Turn right toward the town of Murray, eight miles away.

Two miles from the highway junction, enter the old town of Prichard. Two taverns are all that remains of the town. In Prichard, turn right on the paved road up Prichard Creek. Four miles from Prichard, the dredge piles begin. The dredge piles fill the creekbed for about seven miles around the town of Murray. The piles are mammoth mounds of bare rock created when the gold dredge ripped up everything in the valley floor, washed the dirt and vegetation away, kept the gold, and left nothing but bare rock in its path. Around Murray, a huge bucket-wheel dredge began consuming the valley in 1917 and worked the area through the 1920s.

On the left, one mile after the start of the dredging, a historic marker was placed explaining that A. J. Prichard and his partners found gold near this spot in 1882. By 1884, five thousand miners lived in Murray.

One mile from the marker, the road enters Murray, population of fifty. Murray has an uninviting look, keeping its rough frontier appearance. But for anyone interested in mining, the town is a mandatory stop. The best place to begin is at the Sprag Pole Inn and Museum in the middle of town. Upstairs, smiling from the window, is a model of the renowned local prostitute, Molly B'Dam. Molly's real name was Maggie Hall, and she followed the miners to Murray. During the 1888 smallpox epidemic, her heroism was revealed. While nursing the sick miners, she was stricken and died at the age of thirty-four. She and another well-known local favorite, Terrible Edith, are buried at the local cemetery.

Downstairs, the Sprag Pole combines a tavern, cafe, and museum. Walt Almquist started collecting things in 1962, and never stopped. His museum now fills the Sprag Pole and the building next door. The eclectic collection includes everything from hand-carved wooden chains, to old mining gear, to whiskey kegs, to seashells, to Mike Frank's homemade snow shovel.

A highlight of the visit is a chance to hear a 1904 carnival organ. Pay a quarter at the bar, and the cymbals clang, the drums beat, the organ pipes play, and you can hear two merry tunes. The inn and museum are open daily. The building is not wheel-chair accessible. Admission is free. Contact the Sprag Pole at PO Box 397, Murray, ID 83874, (208) 682-3901.

Across the street and three doors down from the Sprag Pole is the Bedroom Gold Mine Bar. This building opened in 1885 as a grocery store. In 1967, Chris Christopherson bought the store, converted it into a tavern, and then in the bedroom at the back of the building, started digging.

He dug down thirty-two feet until he hit bedrock. Over the next twenty years he dug 180 feet of tunnels, and found plenty of gold that the dredge had missed. His biggest nugget weighed eight ounces. In 1988, he sold the business to his niece for ten dollars. During the summers, he and his family pump the water from the tunnels and dig a little further.

Visitors can see the top of the bedroom mine shaft. The owners will allow anyone to pan for gold in the stream of sand and water that overflows from the mine pumps, for free. Yes, there's plenty of fine gold to be found in that stream. The address is Bedroom Gold Mine Bar, PO Box 395, Murray, ID 83874, (208) 682-4394. The bar is open daily. It is not wheelchair accessible.

The Bedroom Gold Mine Bar is on the corner of the Prichard Creek Road and Forest Road 605. The Murray Pioneer Cemetery is one-half mile down that forest road. One-half mile later, notice on the left the mine tunnel covered with the wooden door. The cemetery is 100 yards past that tunnel on the left, behind a fence. The first burial occurred in 1887. The grounds are well-maintained today. New wooden headstones have recently been placed for several significant historic figures, including A. J. Prichard, Molly B'Dam, and Terrible Edith.

One mile ahead is an overlook pulloff, offering a great view of the dredge piles. After sixty years, those scars have not healed. Five dusty miles ahead, Forest Road 605 connects with the paved road back to Wallace. To avoid the dust, return to Murray, then retrace the paved route back to Wallace.

Finishing The Freeway Tour

To complete the tour, go east on I-90. The town of Mullan, named for the man who built the first road along this route, is eight miles east of Wallace. Then for eight more miles, the Interstate climbs upward to the summit of Lookout Pass at the Montana border, elevation 4,680 feet above sea level.

This tour is over. This journey across the Idaho Panhandle may have taken a few hours, or a few weeks, but hopefully everyone agrees — freeways can be fun.

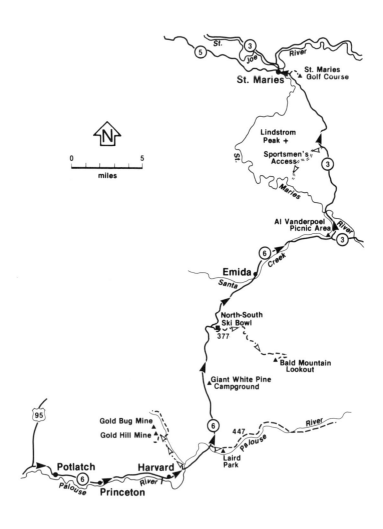

St. Joe Baldy
+

St.

Joe River

5   3

St. Maries
Golf Course

St. Maries

N

0   5

miles

Lindstrom
Peak +

St.

Sportsmen's
Access

3

Maries

Al Vanderpoel
Picnic Area

River

3

6

Creek

Emida

Santa

North-South
Ski Bowl

377

Bald Mountain
Lookout

Giant White Pine
Campground

95

Gold Bug Mine

River

Gold Hill Mine

6

447

Palouse

Potlatch

Laird
Park

Harvard

6

Palouse

River

Princeton

Chapter 8

WHITE PINE DRIVE

(49 miles)

Time: A minimum of one hour by automobile.

Services: Drinking water and restrooms are available at the Harvard city park and at Giant White Pine Campground. A cafe, grocery store and gas station are available at Harvard, Princeton and Emida. All services are available in Potlatch and St. Maries.

Bicycles: White Pine Drive is a difficult, yet lovely, bicycling tour. The highway is paved along the entire length. The road is winding, steep and narrow as it crosses the Palouse Divide at the mid-point of the tour and over the ridge between Mashburn and St. Maries at the end. Along most of the route, the roads do not have wide or paved shoulders. The highway is used extensively by logging trucks, and they can be difficult companions for bicyclists on narrow mountain roads. Water and restrooms are readily available during the first half of the tour, but not in the twenty-five miles from Emida to St. Maries. The tour is beautiful, but suitable only for experienced bicyclists.

Wheelchairs: Unless otherwise indicated, all of the places described in this chapter are wheelchair accessible.

This forty-nine-mile tour follows Idaho Highway 6 from its origin, near the town of Potlatch, to St. Maries. It begins at the edge of the rolling grainfield country known as the Palouse, then follows the Palouse River northward as it becomes a mountain stream. (More information on the Palouse appears in Chapter 1.) The route then crosses into the valley of the St. Maries River, ending at the town of St. Maries. Along the way, the tour passes picture-perfect ranches, with cattle, hayfields, and weathered barns. The tour also wanders through beautiful forestland, including the only accessible forest of old growth cedar and white pine remaining in Idaho. In honor of its beauty, this highway was designated the White Pine Scenic Drive in 1976.

Visitors will notice an absence of several ingredients of contemporary American life while traveling this route. There are no billboards along the road, no stop lights at intersections, and no franchised fast-food eateries. The number of travelers and residents is too small to support such things. Visitors seeking bright lights and billions of burgers will be disappointed. But those who value a peaceful drive through bucolic countryside and majestic forests should enjoy White Pine Drive.

Since it isn't even fifty miles long, visitors can drive its entire length in an hour, but only if they never stop to admire the hawks soaring overhead, to enjoy the two river valleys, or to wander through the forested mountains. At least one day is necessary, to fully savor the White Pine Drive. Those who are interested in camping can stretch their visit to a week or more.

Start The Scenic Drive

The tour begins on Highway 95 about seventy miles south of Coeur d'Alene or forty-five miles north of Lewiston. At the junction of State Highways 6 and 95, turn east on Highway 6. One-half mile ahead, a highway sign on the right provides a map and some introductory information about White Pine Drive. One more half-mile ahead, on the left, is the office of the US Forest Service Potlatch Ranger District. Information about hunting and fishing, or local campgrounds, is available here. A similar district office is in St. Maries. The Potlatch Ranger Station is at Route 2, Box 4, Potlatch, ID 83855, (208) 875-1131. The

St. Maries Ranger District can be contacted at PO Box 407, St. Maries, ID 83861, (208) 245-2531.

Potlatch

One-half mile from the US Forest Service Ranger Station, the tour enters the town of Potlatch. The huge empty field on the right was the site of the Potlatch lumber mill, at one time, the biggest white pine mill in the world. The mill, and the town adjacent to it, were built in 1906 by Potlatch Lumber Company.

A recently-restored, eighty-four-year-old locomotive from the company railway is expected to form the centerpiece for a new park on the right side of the highway. The fourteen-acre park, called Scenic 6 Historical Park, is under development on the Potlatch mill site. Plans include the development of an information center, historical displays, restrooms, and RV hookups. The proposed park will adjoin the Potlatch Lions Club Park.

The forested land to the north and east of the town were once covered with Western White Pine. These trees were especially prized since the wood was light, straight-grained, and strong. The pines were also known for their large size and tall, relatively branch-free trunks. The white pine forest sparked a timber boom early in this century.

Much of that forest was logged off, and most of the rest was killed by the white pine blister rust. The US Government, determined to save the white pines, funded a massive project to kill all the ribes plants throughout their timberland. The ribes, a family of forest bushes that includes the gooseberry, served as an alternate host to the disease. The project was based on the assumption that wiping out the ribes plants would eradicate the rust as well. Thousands of young men, enrolled in the Civilian Conservation Corps, pulled ribes plants, to end the blister rust infestation. With the coming of World War II, and the loss of most of the white pines to rust or to logging, the program ended.

The blister rust is still killing white pines in Idaho, but the US Forest Service has concentrated on locating and breeding a rust-resistant variety. That project was successful, and white pines are again growing strong in Idaho.

99

The Potlatch mill was built in 1906 with state-of-the-art equipment. After the big trees were gone, and the mill outlived its usefulness, it was closed in 1981. After the closure, some feared that the town would disappear too, but it is in surprisingly good economic health, with a population approaching 900. Many residents commute to work in nearby Moscow, Idaho, or Pullman, Washington; others work at smaller mills nearby.

The mill itself was demolished in 1983. Most of the buildings were disassembled, and the wood was saved. Dozens of homes in the region have been constructed or remodeled using the huge timbers originally used to build the cathedral-like mill buildings.

Virtually all of the buildings in Potlatch were built by the company. The large building on the left as you enter the town, at the curve of the highway, is the old company gymnasium. The two boulders in front of the gymnasium are a monument to William Deary, the company's general manager. On the right side of the road is the weather-beaten railroad depot, built for the company-owned Washington, Idaho, and Montana Railroad.

About one-half mile past the old mill site is another beautiful old building that dates from those boom times. The Log Inn is adjacent to the highway, on the right, opposite the cemetery. The logs, some up to two feet in diameter, were hand-peeled and hand-notched by a crew of Scandinavian log carpenters. Construction was begun in 1925 and completed in 1930.

The logs used in the building are all tamarack, the local name for the Western Larch. The Western Larch is an unusual tree, because even though it is a conifer (or evergreen), it acts like a deciduous tree. The larch drops all its needles in the fall after they have changed color. Those visiting this region in autumn will certainly notice the bright yellow-orange color of the larch trees dotting the hillsides.

The Log Inn was built as the American Legion post. The Legion still owns the building, and uses it occasionally for meetings, but it is now a tavern and restaurant. The building is well-maintained and worth a visit to admire the log craftsmanship. A brass plaque on the outside of the black-rock chimney honors World War I veterans.

The Log Inn is open for dinner only, Tuesday through Saturday, and specializes in steaks and seafood. Tables by the windows offer a modest view of the Palouse River to the south and east. For more information, contact Jack and Donna Hash, HC 01, Box 36, Harvard, ID 83834, (208) 875-0109 or (208) 875-1400.

The Potlatch City Park is adjacent to the Log Inn. Camping and picnicking sites are available there under the trees, but no drinking water or restrooms are available there. There is no charge for using the park. Continue the tour on Highway 6 north.

University Cities

Two miles past the Log Inn is the small town of Princeton. It is the first of the "university cities" along the tour. In 1906 and 1907, when this stretch of the Washington, Idaho, and Montana Railroad was built, the villages along the route were named by the college students working on the construction crews.

There were originally eight university cities: Princeton, Harvard, Yale, Wellesley, Stanford, Vassar, Purdue, and Cornell. Those eight, plus Potlatch, Bovill and Deary, were the station stops along the line. When the railroad ceased operation, six of the eight university cities disappeared completely; only Princeton and Harvard remain.

Beyond Princeton, the forest gradually encroaches upon the cultivated fields, the valley narrows, and the grainfields are replaced with hayfields and pastures. The weather in the upper Palouse River valley is too wet and cold for grains, but it is fine for hay. Another ten miles ahead, the farms and ranches disappear as the forest moves right up to the roadside.

Four miles past Princeton, two large lumber mills are on the right. The first is Princeton Lumber Company and the second is operated by Bennett Lumber Products. Half-hour tours of the Bennett mill are available, at no charge, from John Hall, the mill's personnel manager. Visitors should make reservations at (208) 875-1121.

A Herd of Model A's

Garden Gulch Road looks like any other gravelled sideroad, except for the small sign pointing to Idaho Vintage Auto, the antique automobile restoration business owned by Mel and Judy Colvin. The sign welcomes visitors who would like to see Colvin's collection of Model A roadsters and trucks. Mel is proud of his antique autos, and is willing to take a few minutes, if he's not too busy, to show them to visitors.

Mel Colvin bought his first Model A in 1959, when he was twelve years old. The car cost $25 because it was in pieces — and that was the only way he could afford to buy it. But after many hours of work, his Ford was driveable. "I put it together by the time I turned sixteen," Colvin recalled. "And that meant I won the bet with my sister. She bet me ten dollars that I couldn't get it running before age sixteen, and she has never bet with me since then."

Seventeen years ago, Mel bought a 1929 Model A two-door that belonged to his wife's family. It is now the family's touring car. After about $5,000 for parts and materials, plus thousands of hours of labor, it cruises beautifully at about forty-five to fifty miles per hour. The Colvins use the car to travel all over the Northwest. Now Mel and his wife Judy own a half-dozen Model As.

"Touring, not showing, is our enjoyment," he said. "Driving the Model A is fun — people wave and honk, gawking at us — even if they wouldn't give you the time of day otherwise, they are real friendly when we're in the car."

That friendliness is part of their lives and business. Travelers are welcome to visit their shop and see the Model As, at no charge. All they ask is a call in advance, at (208) 875-1448. Their address is Idaho Vintage Auto, Route 1, Box 50, Princeton, ID 83857.

Two miles past the Bennett mill is the village of Harvard, now just a post office and small store surrounded by a cluster of homes. Drinking water and restrooms are available in the town park.

One mile past Harvard, the highway crosses the Palouse River. The gravel road that cuts to the left just before the river bridge is the Jerome Creek Road.

Laird Park

North on Highway 6, two and one-half miles from the Jerome Creek turnoff, note the large sign indicating Laird Park. Laird Park is a US Forest Service campground two miles from White Pine Drive. The road to the campground is paved. Twenty-four campsites have been developed with picnic tables, grills, drinking water, and restrooms. A small dam across the Palouse River creates a tiny swimming lake and beach. A grassy picnic area adjoins the beach.

After passing Laird Park, the forest crowds away the cultivated land, and the road starts winding into the mountains. White Pine Scenic Drive is quickly submerged in the tall timber of the last accessible stand of virgin Western White Pine and Western Red Cedar in Idaho. The trees hugging the roadway are reminders of what all the Bitterroot Mountains looked like a century ago.

Giant White Pine

Four miles past Laird Park, the US Forest Service maintains the Giant White Pine Campground, adjacent to the highway on the right. The campground is aptly named, since it contains Idaho's largest Western White Pine, six feet in diameter and 168 feet tall. The giant, which is protected behind a low wooden fence near the entrance, lives there with a few hundred of its brethren.

Besides the big tree, there are other reasons for stopping. A large hand pump provides cool, tasty well water. Restrooms, picnic tables, and twelve campsites are also provided. Several loop trails leave the campground to wander through the tall trees. A few minutes of walking through the old growth timber provides a glimpse into the past.

Continue the tour by turning right at the entrance. The drive is lined with old growth cedar and white pine trees for the next five miles, until the road crosses the top of the hill and descends into the drainage of Santa Creek and the St. Maries River. (The name of the town and the river is pronounced locally as saint MARYS).

At the top of Palouse Divide, a wide turnout is on the left. The turnout is the starting point for a crosscountry ski trail. Hikers can park there in the warmer months and follow the ski trail westward to the forested peaks nearby.

Optional Sidetrip to Bald Mountain Lookout

to visit a nearby fire lookout, turn right (east) at the top of the divide. The gravel road, forest Road 377, provides access to the North-South Ski Bowl, a downhill ski area one mile from the highway. Forest Road 377 is passable for all vehicles. During the winter ski season, the North-South Ski Bowl offers a hot tub, tavern, restaurant and lodging daily. During the summer, the facility is open on weekends for hikers, huckleberry pickers, and those who enjoy the great view to the north. For more information, contact North-South Ski Bowl, PO Box 190, St. Maries, ID 83861, (208) 245-4222.

Those who continue down Forest Road 377 for ten miles will be rewarded with a visit to the US Forest Service's Bald Mountain Lookout. A lookout tower, which is still used for firewatching during high-danger periods, was built on the treeless mountain. The tower is closed to the public, but a splendid 360 degree view is available at the base of the tower.

To continue the tour, return to Palouse Divide.

Santa Creek Valley

At Palouse Divide, continue north on Highway 6. From the top of the Palouse Divide, White Pine Drive descends into the Santa Creek valley. For the next dozen miles, the tour winds through small ranches and timbered hillsides. It is an idyllic scene. Expect views of cattle in flower-filled meadows and tumbled-down barns at every turn. The tiny town of Emida, five miles from the top of the pass, offers basic services, including a cafe and a convenience store with gas pumps.

The Al Vanderpoel Picnic Area is adjacent to the highway just before the junction with Highway 3. The small recreation area was built by Potlatch Corporation, and is now maintained by the nearby Grange Hall. A half-dozen campsites, plus a tree-shaded picnic area, are provided there. Pit toilets are also offered, but there is no drinking water. Plenty of water to splash and play in is available at Santa Creek, adjacent to the picnic area.

Twelve miles from the top of the divide, Highway 6 ends at its junction with Idaho Highway 3. Turn left on Highway 3.

St. Maries River Valley

Two miles past the junction of Highways 6 and 3, the road crosses the St. Maries River. The large meadow by the river was once the village of Mashburn, and the spot is still known by that name. It is now just a beautiful flower-filled plain surrounded by huge cottonwood trees. The road leaves the river here, rising over a mountain shoulder for the next twelve miles until it returns to the St. Maries River at the town of St. Maries.

From Mashburn, the river winds downstream for twenty miles without any roads along its banks. This is the Canyon of the St. Maries, known locally for the abundance of wildlife along its banks, for its rugged beauty, and for its thrilling rafting opportunities. The St. Maries is shallow, and rafters can run this section only during the high-water season in the spring. The river is dangerous, with long sections of continuous whitewater. Even experienced boaters should be careful. Those who wish to hike into the canyon can follow the railroad tracks. A small parking area on the left, just before the highway begins to rise steeply away from the river, offers access to the river canyon. The parking area is next to the railroad bridge.

Five miles from Mashburn, watch for a Sportsman's Access sign. The Idaho Department of Fish and Game owns Lindstrom Peak and

A Totem With a Tale

Win Applegate, the owner of the St. Joe Sport Shop in St. Maries, wanted a totem pole. His shop, near the western entrance to the town, needed something to attract and welcome visitors. So, Win bought a log, thirty inches in diameter and thirty-three feet long. Then he waited for someone to come by and offer to carve it. Surprisingly enough, someone did.

"One Saturday in August of 1987, a man came into the shop. He was Romanian and spoke very poor English," Applegate said. "He had no wife, just a two-year-old son, and he wanted to sell me the carving in the back of his truck."

Applegate bought the carving, a beautiful crouching Indian with an eagle perched on his head. That sculpture is still in his store, not for sale. "Then I asked him if he wanted to carve my totem pole, and we agreed that I would pay him $500 for the finshed pole," Applegate said. The man, whose name was Anton Dinu, began work the following Monday, using a chainsaw as his only carving tool. By Tuesday afternoon, the totem was complete.

"That Tuesday, I went to pay Anton—and the police came," Applegate recalled. "They wanted to arrest him for assault and battery, for whipping his wife, and Anton grabbed his son, threatening to kill him if the police came closer. I tried to help, I didn't want any harm to come to the boy, so I told Anton that I would take care of his son for him. Anton surrendered. He told me to hold the money until he wrote to me. That night a social worker came to get the boy. Anton told me that he had been a political prisoner in Romania, had been tortured and escaped, came to the US, and ended up in Bonners Ferry, Idaho, married to an American. He said that after she left him, she filed the charges that led to his arrest."

Anton was returned to Bonners Ferry, tried, found guilty, and sentenced to prison. In 1987, Applegate got a letter from Anton requesting that the payment be sent to him at the prison. "I sent him his $500," Applegate said. "Then later the police talked with me — Anton had been sent back to Bonners Ferry to complete his sentence and had escaped from jail. The police thought he might be in Canada, or maybe just living out in the woods, since he was a real survivalist. But I haven't heard from him since he wrote from prison to thank me for the check. He was a strange individual, but he sure had talent."

Visitors are welcome to stop by the St. Joe Sport Shop at Fourth and College Avenues in St. Maries, ID 83861. Phone (208) 245-4417.

Applegate and the totem pole.

thousands of acres of forestland on the left side of the road there. The area is managed for game habitat, and is open for hunting in season. The roads in the hunting area are dirt, and not always passable for all vehicles.

On the left, one-quarter mile past the Sportsman's Access sign, note the homemade mining exhibit at the driveway on the left. A nicely-constructed lifesized mine train and mine tunnel entrance were recently built there.

Ahead, the road begins to descend back into the valley of the St. Maries River. The mountain visible straight ahead is St. Joe Baldy, on the far side of the St. Joe River.

St. Maries

The town of St. Maries is at the bottom of the grade, twelve miles from Mashburn. Just before St. Maries, another Sportsman's Access sign is on the left. This directs visitors to a free boat ramp and dock along the St. Maries River.

One-half mile before town, note the highway sign on the left. The sign points toward the St. Maries Golf Course, three-quarters of a mile to the right on a gravel road. The notation for three-quarters is misplaced on the sign and seems to indicate that the golf course offers three-quarters of a restaurant.

The Broken Tee Lounge is a full restaurant offering the finest dining in St. Maries. The dining room and deck provide a great view of the golf course and the forested hills to the south. The restaurant and tavern are open for weekend dinners and daily lunches during the winter, and lunch and dinner daily in the summer. Contact the Broken Tee Lounge, Rt. 4, Box 6, St. Maries, ID 83861, (208) 245-3842.

Returning to the tour, continue into St. Maries. All services are offered in this town of three-thousand. A free public dock and boat ramp, plus a swimming beach, are available on the banks of the St. Joe River at Aqua Park at the bottom of Tenth Street. Drinking water, picnic tables, and restrooms also are available at the park.

A surprisingly delightful art gallery is operated by the non-profit St. Maries Council for the Arts. The address is 1117 Main Street, St. Maries, ID 83861, (208) 245-3417. The gallery is open, at no charge, Wednesday through Saturday from 10:30 A.M. until 5 P.M. The work of local and regional artists is featured.

St. Maries is surrounded by beautiful Idaho backcountry. Visitors can travel in any direction and find more to see and enjoy. The St. Joe River upstream from town is an officially-designated Wild and Scenic River, home for the native Cutthroat Trout. Some of the finest hunting, hiking and huckleberry picking is found north of town, up St. Joe River Road.

The St. Joe River, downstream from St. Maries is the world's highest navigable waterway. Early in this century, it was the primary transportation route for the loggers, miners, and homesteaders who settled in the Bitterroot Mountains. Today, the river's high banks, filled with huge cottonwood trees, provide a beautiful living canopy for boaters and picnickers.

This is the end of the tour. To reach Highway 95, go west on Highway 5 to Plummer. To reach I-90, continue north on Highway 3.

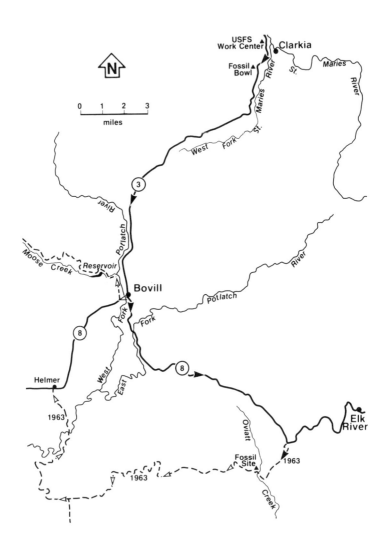

CHAPTER 9

Finding the Fossils

(30 miles)

Time: A minimum of forty-five minutes by automobile.

Services: Restrooms and drinking water are available at the US Forest Service Work Center at Clarkia. Meals, groceries, supplies and gasoline are available at Clarkia and Bovill.

Bicycles: This tour is an excellent route for bicycles. The roads, except for three miles of gravel on Forest Road 1963, are paved and usually have shoulders wide enough for bicycle travel. The road over the one pass is not steep or very winding. However, bicyclists must share the road with trucks hauling logs or wood products.

Wheelchairs: Of the places listed in this chapter, only Buzzard's Roost Trophy Company is wheelchair accessible. Wheelchairs can be brought adjacent to fossil sites for viewing or splitting rock layers.

This tour begins at the US Forest Service's Work Center one-half mile west of Clarkia, Idaho. Clarkia is on Highway 3, about sixty-five miles northeast of Lewiston or about sixty miles south of Coeur d'Alene. The tour follows Highway 3 for fifteen miles to Bovill, continues on Highway 8 toward the town of Elk River, and ends at the Oviatt Creek fossil digging site.

This short tour focuses on Miocene leaf fossils. During the Miocene Era, roughly fifteen million years ago, the climate here was similar to the weather in Florida today. Consequently, the plants growing in the region were different. Instead of today's pine and fir forest, the hills were covered with magnolias, avocados, oaks, maples, and redwoods.

There is another important difference. A large lake filled the valley, and fine silts and clays were washed down from the hills around that lake (known by geologists as Miocene Lake Clarkia). Leaves from the nearby plants floated into the lake, sank, and were covered with layers of eroded silt and clay. During the intervening years, the lake disappeared and the layered lakebottom was compressed and slowly dried.

Today, fossilized Miocene Era leaves, insects, and fish are found in those rocks. The fossils are not difficult to find. What is remarkable about the gathering sites near Clarkia is that the fossils are so abundant and well-preserved. According to Dr. Jack Smiley, the University of Idaho geology professor who is the expert on the site, the Clarkia region is a "world-class fossil locality." Scientists from Asia, Europe, and North America regularly visit the area to study the fossils to better understand the Miocene Era. They come to Clarkia because virtually every rock there has at least one fossil, and because leaves are so well-preserved that the vein structure and even individual cells remain visible today.

The conditions at Miocene Lake Clarkia were so perfect for quick fossilizing that in many cases the original leaf—even though it fell fifteen million years ago—can be carefully lifted from the rock. Some leaves are preserved in their brilliant fall colors (the colors fade quickly to black, however, when the leaves are exposed to air).

Millions of fossils have been removed from the area since it was discovered in 1971. About forty-thousand of the best specimens, representing about four-hundred species, including thirty or forty previously unknown species, are housed at Dr. Smiley's University of Idaho research laboratory, which is not open to the public.

Plenty of fossils remain. The entire upper St. Maries River valley is built on layers of fossil-bearing rock. Visitors who dig for an hour or two can carry home boxes of fossils, including dozens of mantlepiece-quality specimens.

Clarkia

This tour begins at the US Forest Service Work Center near Clarkia. It is on the south side of Idaho Highway 3, about nine miles east of Fernwood and one-half mile west of Clarkia. It is open weekdays from May until October. Drinking water and restrooms are available there. The address is US Forest Service, Clarkia Work Center, Clarkia, ID 83812, (208) 245-2514.

From the work center, the tour heads south on Highway 3. One-half mile later, the highway passes Clarkia on the left, on the other side of the railroad tracks. The large log loading facility adjacent to Clarkia is operated by Potlatch Corporation to sort and load logs from the nearby mountains.

Buzzard's Roost Trophy Company

Two miles from the Work Center, on the right, is a large warehouse, the home of the Buzzard's Roost Trophy Company. The trophy-making factory, and the Fossil Bowl motorcycle racetrack adjacent to it, are owned by the Kienbaum family.

At the factory, the Kienbaums make trophies and plaques for the racers at their track, and for sale nationwide. The shop and warehouse are open to visitors. The Kienbaums give free tours of the facility, if they are not too busy. They ask that visitors contact them before arriving. The address is Buzzard's Roost Trophy Company, 85th and Plum, Clarkia, ID 83812, (208) 245-3608.

Digging Fossils

The Fossil Bowl next door is aptly named. It is the site of the original fossil discovery in the region, and today remains the very best place to dig fossils. The Kienbaums charge five dollars per adult per day to dig fossils. They take visitors to the digging area and describe

The Amazing Kienbaums

In September of 1971, Francis Kienbaum was working sixteen to twenty hours daily, digging stumps, flattening hills, and rounding corners for his new snowmobile racetrack. Winter would soon halt his efforts, so he worked long hours every day. Early one evening he bulldozed into the hillside, to form the north turn of his track. "I hit some dark, slick, gooey stuff there, but I didn't stop to look, I just turned up the gas another notch and pushed on through," he recalled. "We started working on the other side of the track, and it was another week before I got back to that hill."

When he returned to the north turn, he noticed leaves — black leaves, some embedded in rock and some blowing loosely in the wind. They were leaves from the magnolias, oaks, and redwoods that grew there fifteen million years ago. Kienbaum had unearthed a bed of Miocene Era leaf fossils. His family had been living atop those fossils since his father moved to the area forty years before.

Since Kienbaum's discovery, scientists have taken millions of fossils from the cut bank at the north turn. About 40,000 of the best specimens, representing about four-hundred species (including an estimated thirty to forty new species), are stored at the University of Idaho under Dr. Jack Smiley's care.

Declaring that the site was of significant scientific interest, the University of Idaho arranged with Kienbaum to allow continued research there for academic personnel. In exchange, his daughter, Naureen, received a tuition-free education at the University. Because of the abundance of the fossils there, Kienbaum also offered digging rights to others.

The Kienbaums operate Buzzard's Roost Trophy Manufacturing Co. Francis, his wife Vickie, and their son Kenneth love old woodworking equipment and use antique machines to make trophies, plaques, and picture frames. Many

Francis Kienbaum holding a rock showing fossilized leaves.

of their woodworking machines are over one hundred years old, beautifully restored and perfectly functional.

The Kienbaums started making trophies in 1975 because they couldn't afford to buy new ones to give to the winners of motorcycle and snowmobile races at their Fossil Bowl track. Since their trophies are so well made and inexpensive, they started selling them locally, then nationwide. They now sell about five thousand trophies and plaques every year. They are attractively designed, made of stained pine in intricate or plain designs, depending upon their use. With the metal statues and polished wood, the trophies look like the awards given at any track nationwide. No one could tell they were made on century-old equipment.

Those who visit the Kienbaums, to dig fossils or to tour the trophy-making factory, can ask Francis about the family's unusual address, the one painted on the billboard out front— 85th and Plum. Those who don't meet the amazing Kienbaums will have to settle for this explanation: "Well, we're eighty-five miles from Spokane and plum out in the middle of nowhere."

Visiting Bovill

"We love visitors; anybody who comes to Bovill can come to the store to stop and sit," said Karen Eggers. Karen and Maude Carlin work at Hall's Country Store. Maude has lived in Bovill for sixty years, and now works for her son-in-law, Lloyd Hall, the owner of the country store. Karen is a relative newcomer to the area, and is the wife of Bovill's mayor, Gary Eggers.

Their invitation to visitors is a real one. A half-dozen chairs by the front window of the store await travelers, or locals, who want to rest, sip a cup of coffee, chat, and look at the scrapbooks.

Karen has assembled eight big scrapbooks to illustrate the history of this small logging community. The books are filled with photos and mementos. She created the scrapbooks, and wrote a booklet detailing the history of Bovill, because of her fascination with the town's past.

I've lived in Bovill for twenty-seven years. The history of this town interests me. I love this area – the woods, the fresh air, the clean water. Plus I enjoy talking with the Old Timers. It is wonderful to help save this town's history.

In the early 1920s, Bovill was booming. Tall timber surrounded the town, and a railroad delivered the supplies and hauled out the lumber. Bovill was the county's third largest town, with a population of 1,200. Now, like most of the rural logging towns in the Inland Empire, empty buildings and vacant lots testify to the lost residents and the bottomed economy. Bovill's population has dropped to about three hundred.

Without Karen Eggers, much of the glory of Bovill's past might have been lost. Perhaps memories of the two-story outhouse, the woolen mill, and the turpentine factory would have faded away. Everyone might have forgotten that the Elk Tavern was originally the First Bank of Bovill, but with Karen's scrapbooks and history booklet, the past is now preserved.

Maude Carlin and Karen Eggers.

Saving the town's history is the smart thing to do. Learning about their history gives our younger generation a new appreciation of Bovill – they get a new pride in our town as they learn more about it.

Visitors can take a few minutes, or a few hours, to learn some local history. Karen and Maude encourage travelers to sit, to talk, and to enjoy the scrapbooks. Hall's Country Store is open daily on Second Street (the town is too small to worry about street numbers), Bovill, ID 83806, (208) 826-3232.

the digging process. Digging is permissable any day, but weekdays are preferred, since the racetrack is used for motorcycle racing most summer weekends. Contact the Kienbaums at the trophy factory.

The digging is quite easy. The fossils are in finely layered rocks in the hillside adjacent to one of the track's banked turns. Dig into the bank with a shovel or mattock to cut out sections of rock about ten inches on a side. Pull out those hunks of rock and turn them sideways. Note the dozens of fine layers in the brown, tan, or black rock. Insert a knife (a kitchen knife, or sturdy pocket knife is appropriate) between the layers. The rock is soft enough to insert easily. Twist the knife blade, and the layers pop apart. Expect to see a leaf, or possibly an insect, or occasionally even a fish, appear on the split rock.

The rocks are moist and soft. If the specimens are mishandled, the fossil imprints will disappear or the rocks will crumble. Fossils should be wrapped immediately in several layers of newspaper. The paper protects the fossils and allows them to dry slowly, lessening the chances of cracking. As soon as possible, place the rocks in a cool, dry storage area (a basement is ideal). After the fossils have slowly dried, for two or three months, they can be unwrapped and displayed.

Returning to the tour, continue south on Highway 3. The valley of the upper St. Maries River is beautiful. The wide meadowlands adjacent to the road are filled with a succession of blooming wildflowers. The bright blue flowers that appear in June are camas. The forested hillsides adjacent to the valley are home to deer, elk and moose. Wildlife sightings are common along this tour.

About a mile past the Fossil Bowl, the tour leaves the valley and climbs over the saddle into the valley of the Potlatch River. The forest on both sides of the road over the pass is lush and thick, growing right up to the edge of the highway.

Bovill

About fifteen miles from the Fossil Bowl, the tour leaves the forest and enters another wide valley and the small town of Bovill. The town was named for Hugh Bovill, the town's founder and first postmaster. The spot was originally called Warren Meadows, after a local cattleman. Bovill was an Englishman who came to America looking for a natural paradise. He found it when he bought the ranch from Warren in 1899. He then established the Bovill Hotel and a general store. Lumberjacks soon filled the new town and started cutting the huge stands of white pine in the surrounding hills. In 1907, the town incorporated. Boom times came after 1910, when two railroad lines met at the town. Hugh Bovill regretted seeing his paradise ruined by logging, so he sold out and moved to the Coeur d'Alene area to find peace and quiet.

The town has another claim to fame. A herd of twenty-eight elk from Yellowstone National Park were released near Bovill in the 1920s. They were the first elk introduced to North Idaho, and formed the basis for the large wild herds in the area today.

Optional Moose Creek Reservoir Sidetrip

Those who want to sample a local lake can visit Moose Creek Reservoir. From Bovill, follow Highway 3 south toward Deary. A half-mile south of Bovill, turn right on a well-maintained gravel road. The intersection is marked with a Sportsman's Access sign. Follow the road for two miles to the reservoir.

This twenty-acre lake is a local camping, boating, and fishing destination. A free launch ramp and dock are provided. Good fishing for bass and lake trout, both from banks and boats, is available. A small free campground includes pit toilets but no drinking water.

To return to the tour, go back to Bovill.

Oviatt Creek Fossil Locality

The tour continues at the intersection of Highway 8 and Highway 3 in Bovill. Go east on Highway 8 toward the town of Elk River (see Chapter 10 for more information on this area). About eleven miles east of Bovill, turn right onto Forest Road 1963. A large sign identifies this junction. Forest Road 1963 is gravelled and well-maintained, but visitors often share the road with logging trucks, so drive carefully.

Two miles from the highway junction, Road 1963 turns right at a fork. This junction is well-marked. One mile past that fork, watch for the intersection with Forest Road 4704 and the bridge over Oviatt Creek. Just past the bridge, note the exposed hillside on the right. That is the Oviatt Creek Fossil Site. A half-dozen old concrete pillars have been placed along the roadway in front of the hillside digging area.

This is the only place on National Forest land in this area where visitors can legally dig for fossils. Fossil-bearing rock appears else-where in the area, but this is the only permissable digging site. No fee or permit is required, but no power tools can be used.

This site looks quite nondescript, but under the dirt, the rocks hold their secrets. To begin, dig away the dirt, looking for the horizontal layers of tan or brown rock. The fossils are discovered and preserved using the techniques described earlier in this chapter.

The timberland around Oviatt Creek is the mixture of firs and pines characteristic of the area. The hills have been logged one or more times in the last century. The biggest trees are approximately seventy-five years old. Unless a logging crew is working nearby, few vehicles use this road. This is a remote forest site, so no drinking water or restrooms are provided.

A pleasant creekside walk is available on Forest Road 3237, which parallels Oviatt Creek. Forest Road 3237 begins across Forest Road 1963 from the fossil digging site. This road is flat, and provides a pleasant walk along the creek.

This is the end of the tour. Those who wish to return to Highway 8, and then go to either Bovill or Elk River, should retrace their path on Road 1963. Those who want to see more backcountry can continue twenty more gravelled miles ahead on Road 1963, which ends at Highway 3 near Helmer.

CHAPTER 10

OVER THE DENT BRIDGE

(59 miles)

Time: A minimum of two hours by automobile.

Services: All services are available in Bovill, Elk River, and Orofino. Many picnicking and camping areas are scattered along the route, but only Dent Acres has modern restrooms and drinking water.

Bicycles: Only the first twenty miles of this route are advisable for bicycle traffic. Highway 8 (the bicycle-appropriate section of this route) is a paved two-laner with passable shoulders and no long, steep grades. There is some truck and camper traffic, but it is a beautiful biking road. After Elk River, the route is mostly gravelled, narrow and steep. As the road nears Orofino, for the last five miles, the pavement returns, but the roadway is very steep and very narrow.

Wheelchairs: Unless otherwise indicated, all of the places described in this chapter are wheelchair accessible.

This tour begins at the backwoods crossroads of Bovill, Idaho, at the junction of Highways 3 and 8, about fifty miles northeast of Lewiston and about ninety-five miles southeast of Coeur d'Alene. The tour follows Highway 8 for twenty miles, then continues another thirty-nine miles on an improved gravel road to Orofino, thirty-two miles east of Lewiston.

121

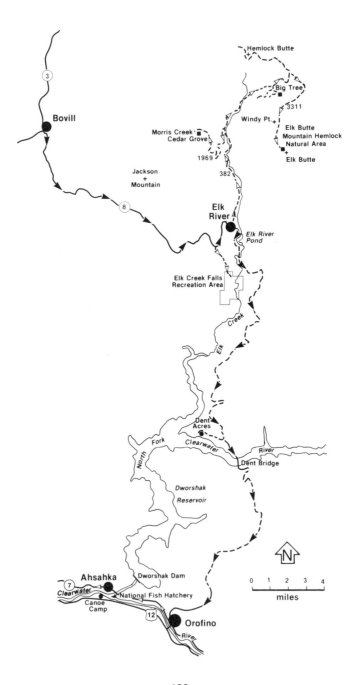

Hemlock Butte

Big Tree

3311

Windy Pt.

Elk Butte
Mountain Hemlock
Natural Area

Elk Butte

Morris Creek
Cedar Grove

1969

382

Bovill

Jackson
+
Mountain

Elk
River

Elk River
Pond

Elk Creek Falls
Recreation Area

Elk Creek

Elk

Dent
Acres

North Fork

Clearwater

River

Dent Bridge

Dworshak
Reservoir

N

Ahsahka

Dworshak Dam

Clearwater

National Fish Hatchery

Canoe
Camp

0 1 2 3 4
miles

Orofino

River

This is a timberland tour which provides access to recreation sites at forest preserves and along waterways. It also offers views of logging activities. These sixty miles can be driven in one day with ease, with time off for sightseeing and picnicking along the way. With overnight stops at the town of Elk River, or at any of the campgrounds and off-the-road camping places, this tour can be extended from a daytrip to a two-week vacation. You could wander this backroad for a week, enjoy it fully, and never stay at the same place twice.

While part of this route is unpaved, it is passable for everything from sedans to motorhomes. The gravelled sections are well-maintained, and no part is too steep or winding for automobiles. But remember, the reality of multiple-use timberland is logging, and that means big trucks kicking up dust and log-loading from piles along the roadside. Most logging activities stop for weekends and holidays. At all other times, be especially careful.

Bovill

Bovill has an interesting past, and a moderately sleepy present, all of which is detailed in Chapter 9. From Bovill, Highway 8 heads east through second- and third-growth forest (meaning it was cut one or two times and has regrown to its present size).

About 1 1/2 miles from Bovill, the highway passes beneath a major electrical transmission line. Power from Dworshak Dam surges north through this line to tie in with the rest of the Northwest's electrical gridwork. This tour ends near that dam.

Seven miles from Bovill, an abandoned railroad right-of-way is visible along the road, first on the left and then on the right. Note especially the remains of a trestle at mile 8. Early in this century, the Chicago, Milwaukee, St. Paul and Pacific Railroad (aka the "Milwaukee line") was the only way to haul loggers in and logs out of Elk River. On parts of the main Milwaukee line, the locomotives were powered by electricity, but steam trains were used on this spur. The tracks were removed long ago.

Elk Creek Falls

Fifteen miles from Bovill, a large US Forest Service sign announces Elk Creek Falls, the first of many scenic attractions along this route. A well-maintained gravel road cuts to the right off the highway, winding about 2 1/2 miles to the parking lot at road's end.

From the parking area, it is an easy half-mile walk to Elk Creek Falls, the tallest waterfall in North Idaho. Elk Creek has gouged a deep cut in the black basalt bedrock and in three separate drops, cascades a total of three-hundred feet. The falls are worth at least a short visit.

A network of hiking trails (or in winter, cross-country ski tracks) wander under the trees to the three overlook sites above each of the three falls. Those ledges are prime picnic sites. Above the upper falls in the warmer months, creekside diners and freshwater waders can find plenty of grassy patches and shallow pools.

The future of the falls remains in doubt. Investors, hoping to develop the site for hydroelectric power, want to build a dam above the upper falls and pipe water to a generator below the lower falls. This controversial project has been proposed for many years. The US Forest Service wants to maintain the falls as a recreational area, and has denied a construction permit for this project. The developers are trying to gain the approval of other federal agencies. A final decision is likely years away.

Elk River

Return to Highway 8, and turn right (east). Within three miles, the pavement ends at Elk River – a town barely big enough for a stop sign. The townsite was cleared in 1909. Before that, it was just another flat spot along Elk Creek, filled with big trees, mostly valuable Western White Pine, the foundation of North Idaho's turn-of-the-century lumber boom. Potlatch Lumber Company built the mill, and the town, in 1910. At that time, it was the biggest all-electric lumber mill in the US.

During its heyday, about 1930, the population of Elk River topped one-thousand. Now, the population is about 180. After the last mill closed in 1980, another timber town faced an uncertain future.

Many locals are now hoping for an influx of visitor dollars to offset the loss of timber-based income. Four inns of varying sizes and levels of rustic comfort offer accommodations to travelers, hunters, anglers, and skiers. The town is surrounded by an abundance of noteworthy outdoor attractions, scattered throughout the Clearwater National Forest.

The Big Tree

One of the most interesting sites is the Big Tree, which is only ten miles north of Elk River. This giant Western Red Cedar is more than eighteen feet in diameter, taller than a fifteen-story building, and at least three-thousand years old. It's the largest tree in North America east of the Cascade/Sierra Nevada mountains. The huge cedar was discovered in 1979 by two US Forest Service engineers who were surveying a proposed forest road.

The big cedar stands in a wide, wet valley. An intermittent stream flows under and through its base, and a tangle of ferns and alders surround it, keeping the competing trees about one-hundred feet away. The giant's grove is not dense, with a ring of other large cedars standing at a respectful distance.

The road and trail to the Big Tree is plainly marked. Travel north from Elk River on Forest Road 382. The creekside meadows along this route are prime habitat for deer and elk. Be watchful, especially during the morning and evening hours. After ten miles, turn right on Forest Road 4763. The junction is marked with a sign directing visitors to the Giant Cedar. Road 4763 curves to the east for about one mile, until it dead-ends at two gates.

Park near the left gate. The Big Tree is a half-mile hike past that gate and the wooden sign-in shelter. The trail is not wheelchair accessible. This is a good place for a picnic, but restrooms and drinking water are not available here. Walk around the base of the tree and peek into the hole on the south side of the trunk for a glimpse of the stream flowing through its root system.

Andre Molsee

Most towns in North Idaho have long depended on logging for their livelihood. At one time, thousands of men living in these small towns worked as loggers or millhands. Recently, declining harvests and increasing mechanization have closed mills and logging camps. The unemployed workers, their families, and then the shopkeepers who depended on their trade, all moved away. The towns dwindled and some disappeared completely. But some towns are determined to survive, and are finding a new economic base in tourism.

Andre Molsee is a small town businessman who sees a new opportunity in travelers' dollars. As manager and part owner of Huckleberry Heaven Lodge, he's working to help Elk River succesfully survive that transition from logging to tourism.

He looks a little like the Marlboro Man, the typical Western cowboy, as he rushes around the lodge. He works long hours, greeting customers, loading rental canoes, or finishing some plumbing or carpentry, but it's always with a smile.

Molsee was the superintendent of Elk River's one-school system from 1980 until 1984. While serving as superintendent, he and his wife Nadine joined in partnership with Ethel Lovell, the owner of the town's small grocery store. With an investment of $300,000, the three partners remodeled the store and created Huckleberry Heaven Lodge. They now rent rooms and condominiums, lead fishing and hunting expeditions, and sell supplies and sundries to visitors.

"Our original goal was to create jobs here, to give young people a reason to stay," said Molsee, forty-four. Andre and Nadine were hoping to offer the possibility of a decent living for their own children (three boys and two girls aged eight to seventeen) and the children of their neighbors. Their business success has created jobs for five people during the busy hunting season.

Amon, Andre, and Laban Molsee.

Molsee's determination to make his lodge a travelers' destination helped keep Elk River on the map. He advertises locally, regionally, and nationally—bringing travelers from Spokane, Seattle, and the East Coast. As satisfied customers return or tell others, his business has grown at the enviable rate of twenty percent annually for the last five years. Due to his vision and efforts, the town of Elk River is now known as a place that welcomes travelers.

Not everyone is happy with the change, as Molsee readily admits. Some old-timers cling to their recollections. But with the local lumber mills closed, and four inns now operating there, the economic shift is undeniable. Elk River is not unique, Molsee insists. Many tiny Idaho mill towns could duplicate their success. The key is a dedicated, family-run business, led by people willing to take risks and plan imaginatively.

Morris Creek Cedar Grove

Another cedar forest preserve, Morris Creek Old Growth Cedar Grove, is nearby. To reach Morris Creek Cedar Grove, go south on Road 382 (returning toward Elk River). About five miles from the Big Tree turnoff, Forest Road 1969 makes a sharp right, heading west. The road is clearly marked. After four miles, the road enters a wide valley, and on the left is a tiny sign promising a cedar grove at the end of the trail. A quarter-mile-long trail, which is not wheelchair accessible, leads to the Morris Creek grove. This eighty-acre preserve contains a pure stand of three- to six-foot diameter cedars. The cedars cover a gentle north-facing slope adjacent to the creek. The undergrowth is primarily Mountain Maple, and the autumnal contrast of the yellow maple leaves and the feathery cedar boughs is joyful indeed. But anytime, actually, is a good time to visit Morris Creek.

Campgrounds with primitive facilities are available in the Clearwater National Forest surrounding Elk River. In addition, dispersed camping is allowed in virtually all the forestland there. That means that any flat spots off the road and off the creeks are OK for tent or RV camping. You just pick an agreeable spot and set up camp. The exceptions are the Natural Areas, but that leaves plenty of choices. Of course, no facilities are available at the dispersed campsites.

When choosing a campsite or hiking throughout this area, watch for huckleberries. From early summer at the lower elevations, to late fall on the mountaintops, the berries ripen to purple sweetness. They grow on bushes one to three feet tall in sunny places. The berries are round and about one-quarter of an inch in diameter. No permits are required to pick non-commercial quantities. They are delicious right off the bush, or baked in pies, muffins, and pancakes.

Elk River

When you are finished visiting the big trees, return to Elk River, where a variety of visitor services await you. Huckleberry Heaven is the largest lodge, equipment rental, and convenience store in Elk River. Their huckleberry ice cream is purple and huckleberry-ish. Huckleberry Heaven is on Main Street across from the Post Office.

The lodge is not designed for wheelchairs. The address is PO Box 165, Elk River, ID 83827, (208) 826-3405.

Across the street from the lodge are the town's two, free tennis courts. The courts are lighted, if you can find someone who remembers where to find the switch.

Morris Drug Store is on the opposite corner of the downtown intersection. Thomas and Connie Morris run the business, which began in 1910, the year the town began. William Morris, Thomas' grandfather, ran the pharmacy then, and his brother Harry owned the hardware store. They shared a building built by their father, C. G. Morris, at the site of the present post office. In 1918, the business moved to the present location when William Morris bought the building and the business of a competing drug store.

The new home of Morris Drug includes a marble soda fountain, which is still in use. The white marble beauty is complete with the silver-plated working parts and ornate mirrored cabinetry that was standard equipment when the fountain was hauled to town in 1915. The sodas are delicious, and cheap, but the malts are a great choice too.

After sipping a soda at the fountain or the tables, more nostalgia is available. Seven original, wood-with-beveled-glass display cases fill the small store, which now sells everything from hardware to hard liquor. Against the back wall, one case displays spectacles, remedies, and implements from the old store. Old drug bottles and historic photographs line the high shelves around the interior of the store. Morris Drug is as close as Elk River gets to a museum. The phone number is (208) 826-3407.

When it's time to leave Elk River, go south toward Orofino and the Dent Bridge. It's thirty-nine miles to Orofino and twenty-five of them are unpaved.

Just outside Elk River, past the site of the original lumber mill, is a delightful mountain lake called Elk River Pond. In 1988, a new dam replaced the log dam built by the Potlatch Lumber Company almost eighty years earlier. Potlatch dammed Elk Creek to produce a log pond for their mill. The pond now serves as a recreation site. Four free

The Wildman of the Clearwater

Bill Moreland, the Wildman of the Clearwater, was one of the more famous residents of the backwoods between Bovill and Orofino. He spent thirteen years, from 1932 to 1945, alone in the wilderness of Central Idaho, avoiding all human contact. He slept in caves, hollow trees, and makeshift shelters by day and travelled by night, gliding unseen along game trails. Living like a human coyote and outwitting his pursuers, he was captured only after a determined manhunt spanning several years.

The legend began with the evidence that someone was visiting isolated cabins and Forest Service work camps, taking an occasional pair of socks or tin of food. The legend grew when local woodsmen tried unsuccessfully to track and catch him. The Wildman, gifted with extraordinary cunning and woods-sense, was reputed to be invulnerable to capture.

The US Forest Service was determined to stop his pilferage. They suspected he was an escaped murderer named Baldy Webber. Two outstanding local woodsmen, Moton Roark and Lee Horner, were hired to capture him. Roark and Horner planned their campaign well. They set out after a mid-winter storm, when the snow would reveal the Wildman's tracks and when the clear skies would show any campfire. After a week of slogging through some of the roughest country in Idaho, they saw his camp smoke, circled downwind and surrounded him. They did not catch a heavily-armed murderer, but a meek and agreeable man, five feet two inches tall. On the long hike back to the Canyon Ranger Station, they had plenty of time to talk — and after thirteen years, the Wildman had a lot to say.

In 1932, Moreland explained, he was a homeless drifter who left his native Kentucky looking for a job. Finding no work, he ended up taking his pocketknife and bedroll into the Idaho wilderness. The longer he stayed and the more he pilfered from government cabins, the more convinced he became that he was in danger. Finally, Moreland decided that if he surrendered, he would be killed.

To his captors, the Wildman revealed the mysterious ways he eluded those who tried to find him. He was always on the move, and after thirteen years had developed a network of caves, hollow trees, and caches of supplies from the Montana side of the Bitterroot Crest to the St. Joe River and throughout the Clearwater country. He travelled only at night, when other human traffic on the trails disturbed the game and warned him of danger. Often, he avoided trails entirely, walking a few hundred yards parallel to the established route.

When chased, Moreland often headed for water, either to walk in to cover his tracks or to fool his pursuers with his "double raft" trick. He made many simple rafts, and left one tied on each bank of a river. Instead of crossing the river, he would destroy the raft on his side, then hide. Then he would watch his pursuers cross the river, certain the Wildman was over there, since a raft was in plain sight on the far bank. Moreland also confounded his pursuers by leaving a variety of tracks. He carried several pairs of boots, to change his tracks. Sometimes he mounted large boots on poles and used the the bigger footwear, pointing backwards, to cover his own tracks. His most clever ruse left many trackers totally dumbfounded. His trail would go into the center of a clearing, and vanish. The explanation was simple. At the center of the clearing, he would slip on short stilts with elk hooves on the bottoms, and walk away.

Moreland was judged sane, pled guilty to burglarizing Forest Service cabins, and spent eight months in jail. Upon his release, he spent the next nineteen years living in the small towns along the Clearwater. He worked intermittently at various forestry jobs, and was committed several times to the State Mental Hospital at Orofino. In 1964, at age sixty-three, Moreland escaped from that institution, and was last seen walking up the trail toward Pierce, vowing to leave Idaho because the woods had become too populated.

campgrounds are scattered around the lake. None of these lakeside sites provide utility hookups or drinking water, but improved RV campsites are available in Elk River. A twenty-unit, full-hookup RV park, owned by Huckleberry Heaven Lodge, is in a meadow on the right side of the road between the town and the pond.

A free boat launch ramp and dock are available at Jarvis Park, the campground closest to town. There are no restrictions against power boating, and the twenty-five-acre lake is open for fishing year-round. The lake is stocked regularly, and sixteen-inch brook trout are not uncommon.

About two miles south of Elk River, the road crosses Elk Creek. Elk Creek Falls are about three-quarters of a mile downstream from this point, but no trails are cut along the creek in that direction. Three miles from town, a gravel road cuts sharply to the left — looping back around the lake to town again.

To Dworshak Reservoir

The road ahead is a long and winding one, with logging roads angling off in all directions through the timberland. The main road is always obvious, and there are signs pointing toward Orofino. Sixteen miles from Elk River, atop the ridge, there's a glimpse of Dworshak Reservoir off to the right. An overlook area on the right eighteen miles from Elk River offers splendid views of Dworshak Reservoir and the surrounding mountains.

The reservoir was created in 1973 by the impoundment of the North Fork of the Clearwater River behind Dworshak Dam. Its fifty-three-mile length is an open path into what had previously been some of Idaho's most inaccessible backwoods. More than 140 "Mini-Camps" have been built by the US Army Corps of Engineers along the shoreline, with access by boat only. Set in isolated coves and pockets, these single-site camping areas offer only a pit toilet, table, grill, and ample serenity. In addition, scattered around Dworshak's 183 miles of shoreline, the Corps of Engineers also created a handful of modern camping places. One of those big campgounds, Dent Acres, is ahead.

As the road drops down the hill past the overlook, it crosses the National Forest boundary. At the twenty-mile mark, the road forks. Dent Acres is 1 1/2 miles to the right, just past a small country store. Dent is one of the modern tidy camping areas maintained by the Corps of Engineers for those who like camping with the amenities — hot showers, mowed campsites, concrete boat ramp, flush toilets and all. Dent looks like a typical, yet totally transitory, mini-city in a beautiful lakeside setting.

To continue the tour, return to the main road and turn south. In 1 1/2 miles the road leads down to the water's edge and the Dent Bridge. The bridge, which looks like a miniature Golden Gate Bridge, provides a wonderful walkway (on the sidewalk, of course) across the reservoir with great views of the water and the mountains.

Seven miles south of the bridge, the road tops the ridge and offers a splendid view of the Clearwater River valley. From this point, the route to Orofino drifts through eight miles of well-trimmed hay fields and pastures, separated by ribbons of pine trees. It's a scene reminiscent of the Alps or perhaps Scandinavia. For the last several miles, the road drops down a steep grade into Orofino at the valley floor. That's the end of this journey, but the adventure continues.

Orofino

A good place to begin is at the Clearwater County Historical Museum in a small house at 315 College Avenue. The local historical society has gathered logging and mining machinery and household memorabilia from Orofino's past to fill the museum. No fee is charged.

133

The museum is open daily, except Sunday and Monday, from 1:30 to 4:30 P.M. Wheelchair access is not provided.

Picnics are possible, and pleasant, at Kiwanis Park, near the corner of Johnson Avenue and First Street. The park is on the east bank of Orofino Creek. Picnic tables, drinking water, and plenty of shade trees are available at this small park, but no restrooms are provided. A wooden sign across the bridge, about twenty yards from the park, explains the history of Orofino and the Canada Hill District. The town was founded in 1898, after the gold rush up the Clearwater River slowed and the railroad arrived. The name, Orofino, means "fine gold" in Spanish and was borrowed from a small town upriver that had burned down several years earlier. Until the turn of the century, the economic base for the area was gold mining. The gold did not last, and logging became the main industry. Today logging and tourism form the economy of the region.

Fish Hatchery

Many travelers come to the area for the fishing. The most notable local fish are steelhead, an ocean-going rainbow trout that returns to the area annually. There are some naturally-spawning steelhead and salmon, but most of the fish are returning to their man-made birthplace, Dworshak National Fish Hatchery. To find the hatchery, turn west (right) from Orofino onto State Highway 7. At the small cannon park on the north bank of the Clearwater River in Orofino, turn right and travel two miles to the hatchery.

This is the largest steelhead-producing hatchery in the world, raising more than four million fish every year. The facility was opened in 1968, before the dam was completed, to offset the wild steelhead and salmon runs that would be eliminated by the dam. There are eighty-four ponds at the hatchery where adult steelhead and salmon are kept, and where their offspring are raised.

The hatchery is open daily, for free, self-guided tours. The tour begins at the display area by the entrance and continues by following the fish painted onto the pavement.

Dworshak Dam

Three miles past the hatchery on Highway 7 is the Dworshak Dam Visitor Center. The dam, the highest straight-axis concrete gravity dam in the Western World, is adjacent to the Visitor Center. The tour includes a visit inside of the dam as well as the slide shows and historic displays at the center. For more information about the hatchery or about fishing, boating, and camping on the Reservoir, contact the US Army Corps of Engineers, PO Box 48, Ahsahka, ID 83520, (208) 476-3060.

From the entrance to Dworshak Dam, return to Orofino on Highway 7. At Cannon Park at the entrance to town, turn right and cross the bridge over the Clearwater River. This road ends at Highway 12. Turn right (West) on Highway 12 to continue the tour.

Down Highway 12

The Clearwater National Forest Supervisor's Office is on Highway 12, three miles west of Orofino. It can supply information about river or forest use in the region. The address is USFS Supervisors Office, Route 4, Orofino, ID 83544 (208) 476-4541.

A mile west of the Forest Service office is Canoe Camp, a grassy picnicking and fishing area. From September 26 to October 7 of 1805, this was the home of the Lewis and Clark Expedition. Here they cut trees and hollowed the logs into canoes for the long float to the Pacific. Their journey was far from complete, but this ends our tour, the one that began sixty backwoods miles ago in Bovill.

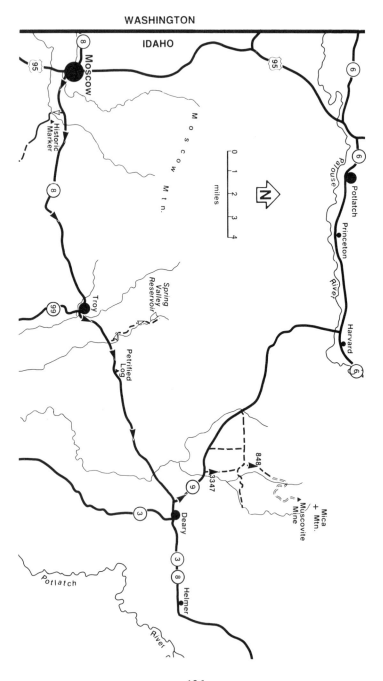

Chapter 11

MOSCOW TO THE MUSCOVITE

(33 miles)

Time: A minimum of 1 1/2 hours by automobile.

Services: All services are available in Moscow and Troy. No other services are available along the tour.

Automobiles: The last six miles of this tour are on rough mountain roads that are impassable to low-slung cars. The first twenty-six miles follow modern, paved roads and a few stretches of good gravel roads.

Bicycles: For the first twenty-six miles of this tour, the highways are paved, flat, and generally have paved shoulders. Highway 8 is well-travelled and the passing traffic makes cycling dangerous, so bicyclists must be careful. The last six miles is not paved, and as the road ascends the mountain, it becomes narrower, steep, and winding. The last six miles of the tour is not recommended for bicyclists, though experienced mountain bike riders will find the road challenging.

Wheelchairs: All the facilities described in this chapter are wheelchair accessible, unless otherwise indicated.

You Can Pet This Dragon

When Mark Solomon bought his 1955 GMC two and a half ton truck, he had some unusual ideas about the vehicle — he wanted to build a dragon. He removed the cab and reinforced the truck's flatbed. Next, he transformed the front half of the truck into a dragon's head. Working from a sketch and cardboard models, Solomon welded steel bracing to the existing frame, and started adding pieces of fourteen-gauge steel plate. He would weld on a plate, beat it into shape, then add another steel sheet. After the dragon's head was complete, lights, turn signals, windows, doors, and a dashboard were installed.

The truck had its debut at the Moscow Renaissance Fair, on May 17, 1980. Solomon's Dragon was an immediate hit with fairgoers. Adults were fascinated, and discussed its construction and inspected its workmanship. Children were excited, and found the Dragon's long sloping nose to be a great playground. Everyone was amazed when the Dragon breathed fire. A propane jet, ignited by an auxiliary spark plug system, spit a two-foot-long flame from the open mouth. The following day, May 18, 1980, Mount St. Helens blew up. "I knew then that the Dragon was going to have an interesting life," Solomon said.

"This truck acts like a magnet for bizarre expressions, and sometimes I wonder if I need liability insurance for all the people who seem to get whiplash from turning their heads so fast," he added. "I use the Dragon as a barometer of how often people smile—and they seem to smile when they see it everywhere, except in Utah, they didn't smile there too often. "Whenever we stop for gas, people come over to talk."

The two most common questions are:

1. What kind of motor does it have? It is a 327-cubic-inch engine from a junked Chevrolet Impala. The Dragon recently received a five-speed transmission from a 1979 truck.

2. Has this ever been on TV? Yes, during the 1980 election, Idaho Senator Frank Church and Idaho Governor John Evans gave campaign speeches from the back of the Dragon. The CBS-TV crew at the rally filmed the fire-breathing mechanism in action. The Dragon appeared briefly on the CBS Evening News the following evening.

The two questions people don't often ask are:

1. How much did it cost, and is it for sale? The truth is that except for perhaps two hundred dollars for used parts and steel, it required no capital outlay—only six months of hard work. It is not for sale, and he doesn't really think anyone can afford to pay him what it would take to build a duplicate.

2. Does the truck have a name? Yes, he calls it Hunter, for the American writer of outrageous social commentaries, Hunter S. Thompson. He named it for one of Thompson's more famous lines: "When the going gets weird, the weird turn pro."

Solomon often parks the truck in front of Idaho Forge and Fabrication, his blacksmithing shop, at 1020 South Main Street in Moscow. He doesn't mind if people examine or photograph the dragon.

This tour begins in Moscow, Idaho. Moscow is on Highway 95, about ninety miles south of Coeur d'Alene and thirty-five miles north of Lewiston.

The entire tour is in Latah County, the only county in the US to be created by an act of Congress. In 1888, the county was established between the borders of the Coeur d'Alene and Nez Perce Indian Reservations. The area was settled by gold miners in the 1860s (for a tour of a local mine, see Chapter 8). Traders and homesteaders followed, establishing towns, plowing the meadows and cutting the forests. About seventy percent of the county is now under cultivation.

The name Latah (pronounced LAY-tah) roughly translates from the Nez Perce language as the "place of pine trees and pestles." The western edge of the county was a grassland where the blue-flowered camas lily grew in profusion. The Nez Perce harvested the camas bulbs and ground them with a mortar and pestle into camas flour. To the Nez Perce, the area offered both forest and camas, and thus their name "Latah."

Moscow, with a population of about seventeen-thousand, is the largest city in the county. The town, was settled in 1869, and was originally called Paradise Valley. It was unofficially known as Hog Heaven, because pigs grew fat eating the camas bulbs.

The name Moscow was adopted in 1875, but its source remains in dispute. Some think it was named for a farming town in the Eastern US. Others suggest it was named for the Russian city. Whatever the source, the name stuck, and remained, despite efforts during the Cold War to change it to a "pro-American" name.

When the state of Idaho was formed, the citizens of the Panhandle were reluctant to join with southern Idaho to form a state. The northerners preferred to join Washington, or form a separate state. To appease them, in 1889, the University was placed in the north, on donated land west of town.

From Moscow

From the southern end of Moscow, follow Highway 8 east toward Troy. This route winds through the Palouse hills, in a wide valley, with Tomer Butte and Paradise Ridge on the right and Moscow Mountain and the Thatuna Hills on the left. The valley was filled with the molten black basalt rock that flowed into the entire Columbia Basin area between six and seventeen million years ago. The hills on both sides are older granite mountains, created about sixty-eight million years ago. As the highway continues east, the grainfields disappear, to be replaced with forestland.

Two miles from Moscow, Lenville Road crosses the highway. The intersection is well-marked. Turn right on Lenville Road. One mile from the highway, visitors will find an unusual monument.

A large boulder is adjacent to the road, on the left side. Mounted on that rock is a brass plaque noting that this spot marked the junction of two ancient Indian trails. Near this point, the Greater Nez Perce Trail came from the east and met the Red Wolf Trail coming from the south. The trails then connected to go north to the Spokane Falls fishing and trading grounds. The brass plaque also records that Washington Territory's first Governor, Isaac Stevens, followed the Red Wolf Trail past this point in June of 1855. Stevens noted that the valley was filled with Nez Perce Indians harvesting camas bulbs. This was the first written record of the Palouse region. The monument was placed here by the Worthwhile Club in 1938. The club is an organization of farm wives living in the area. The club's membership has dwindled to ten members who continue to meet monthly.

To continue the tour, retrace the route to the highway. Cross Highway 8 on Lenville Road to visit the University of Idaho's Plant Science Farm. The large state-of-the-art tree nursery and experimental farm adjacent to the highway here is open for free guided tours on weekdays from 8 A.M. to 5 P.M. Reservations for the tour must be made in advance by calling (208) 885-6499.

Gypo Loggers and Lumberjack Pride

Logging is the economic mainstay of the eastern and northern portions of the Inland Empire. Most of the people who cut the trees, saw them to length, and haul them to the mills are gypos. Gypos (JIPP-ohs) are independent contractors, or the employees of independent contractors. They do not draw salaries, but are paid only for what they produce.

"I've worked my entire life under the gypo system," Bernal Zimmerman noted with pride. "I started at sixteen, a high school dropout, working in the woods with my Dad, near here, around Kendrick. Gypos are paid only what they deserve, only what they earn; there's no guarantees."

Zimmerman's first job was driving a 1937 Caterpillar Model 22 tractor to cut roads and pull logs. He started his own business in 1968, when he was twenty-eight years old. Today, Zimmerman Logging employs about fifty people and contracts with the local mills and timber owners to cut and haul their logs. The 1937 Cat that he operated as a teenager is on display in front of his company headquarters on Highway 8, six miles east of Troy. Other items on display include a 1930's road grader, an ancient log-hauling truck, and a log sled.

He recently expanded his collection to include artwork. He started with an eight-foot-tall statue of a lumberjack, carved from a cedar log. Then he added a carved eagle with outstretched wings. The result is a small, well-kept roadside museum, an attractive display of local history and gypo pride. Visitors are welcome. "I don't mind people stopping by, and getting close to the decorations," he said. "I like to see families out together."

His family has been important to his success, and to the survival of his business during the hard times. "My family is the main ingredient in my life," he said. "It's always a battle, but when your family is behind you, encouraging you, you can keep going." He and his wife, Karen Marlene, raised two children. Their seventeen-year-old son works there part-time.

Zimmerman explained some of the cutting systems used to get the trees out. When the trees are big enough to harvest, the forest is either clearcut or selectively cut.

> A clearcut is managed like a wheat crop. The trees are all the same age, so there's not enough young trees growing to worry about, so we elect to cut them all.

The result of clearcutting are the open treeless areas visible on forested mountainsides. After the logs are removed, the remaining brush and waste wood is often burned. That clears the land for replanting with small tree seedlings.

When forests are not clearcut, they are selectively cut, he continued. "Any time we take out some of the trees, it's a selective cut." When the forest contains both young and old trees, the loggers remove most of the big trees, leaving some for shade and reseeding. This is called a shelterwood cut. Several years later, when the younger trees are well-established, they remove the big trees, which is called overstory removal. The choices of logging system and of specific trees to cut, are made by foresters trained in woodland management and ecology.

> Our forest practices now have come a long way in protecting the forest, since I started. Sometimes it seems like environmentalists and the forest industry can never agree, but we have all come a long way — everybody is working hard now for our future forests.

Troy

Returning to the tour, continue east on Highway 8. Ten miles past Lenville Road, the highway enters Troy, population 860. Troy was settled in 1885, and was originally called Heff's Gulch. The town was built along the Nez Perce Trail. A railroad to Troy was opened in 1890, arranged by a John P. Vollmer, Lewiston banker, who renamed the town after himself. The banker was not well-liked, however, and at an election held six years later, the town was renamed Troy. Local rumor explains that a Greek-born merchant offered free whiskey to all who would vote for his favorite Greek city.

Leave Troy, following Highway 8 toward Deary.

Optional Sidetrip To Spring Valley Reservoir

On Highway 8, about two miles from the junction of Highway 8 and 99, at the east end of Troy, note the small sign marking the entrance to Spring Valley Reservoir. Turn left at the sign, and follow the road for three miles. The entrance road is paved for two miles and then turns to a well-maintained gravel road which is suitable for all vehicles.

Spring Valley is a popular fishing and swimming lake stocked regularly by the state Fish and Game Department. Motorized boats are not allowed on the lake. There are two docks and a primitive launch ramp for rowboats and canoes. The lake is lovely, surrounded by forested hills and rolling hayfields. Several small islands offer great destinations for swimmers. Picnic tables and pit toilets are provided. Camping is free, but no drinking water is available. Though Spring Valley is the most heavily-used park in the county, it is never too crowded for a picnic, a swim, or even an overnight visit.

To return to the tour, retrace the route to Highway 8 and turn left toward Deary.

Following The Highway

About 1 1/2 miles east of the Spring Valley Road junction, the highway makes a gentle curve to the left. Pull onto the shoulder and examine the roadcut on the inside (or left) side of the curve. This hill reveals much of the geological history of the region. Beginning at the road level, note the layers of basalt rock in the exposed hillside. The molten basalt arrived intermittently over an eleven-million-year period. Fissures in the earth periodically opened and lava flowed out, an estimated 150 different times. Between the eruptions, dirt washed down from the mountains, allowing plants to grow in the valley. Eventually, the plants and soil were buried under a new flow of basalt, and the cycle continued. A silicified log remains at this spot as evidence of those times between the basalt flows.

Geologists believe that the silicified log was a sweet gum tree growing on a sandy riverbank about ten million years ago. Molten basalt covered the tree so quickly that it did not burn, but was petrified or silicified. Millions of years later, road construction removed the basalt layer above, revealing the log. The wood is now a slimy-wet, olive-green, clayish rock. It is exposed in the hole at the top of the first short bank inside the middle of the curve of the highway. On close inspection, the grain of the wood is still visible in the rock. Trails to the silicified log are not wheelchair accessible.

Above the basalt, near the top of the roadcut, note the layer of white clay. It was left in a channel cut in the basalt by water flowing from the nearby mountains. The white clay was carried downstream from the mountains. Above the clay, the hill is covered with a rounded layer of wind-blown loess soil. (For information about the Palouse hills and the loess soils, see Chapter 1.)

The tour continues on Highway 8 for seven miles past the silicified log. Just before the town of Deary, turn left onto Highway 9. Highway 9 follows the mountain shoulders northward. On the left are beautiful views of the cultivated fields in the foreground and the forested heights of Moscow Mountain in the back. On the right is Mica Mountain, the destination of this tour.

Up Mica Mountain

About two miles from the intersection of Highways 8 and 9, turn right onto Forest Road 3347. The junction is signed. Cross over the railroad tracks on the one-lane wooden bridge and follow the road east toward the mountain. Forest Road 3347 begins as a well-maintained gravel road, but as it climbs, it narrows and becomes quite rutted. The first two miles of the road provide pleasant views of the forest. Then the road becomes rough and is unsuited for automobiles and bicycles.

Little traffic uses the Mica Mountain Road. More likely is sharing the road with wildlife. Deer and elk, plus hawks, bear, and other creatures call this forest home. The area is regularly logged. Numerous hauling roads fork from the main route, but unless noted here, always follow the obvious well-traveled roadway.

Two miles from the intersection at Highway 9, Forest Road 3347 turns right to Vassar Meadows. The intersection is well-marked. At that junction, continue straight ahead. About one-quarter of a mile later, turn right onto Forest Road 3848. The main gravelled road continues to the left at this intersection, but the tour follows the narrower dirt road on the right.

Low-slung automobiles and bicycles should turn around at this point. Travellers can retrace their route to Moscow, or continue ahead on Highway 9.

For those continuing the tour, after driving about one mile on Forest Road 3848, note the outcrops of mica schist on the roadcuts to the left. Flakes of mica are imbedded in the dark rock, giving them a shiny and sparkling look. As the tour nears the top of the ridge, notice the lovely views of field and forest below on the right.

About five miles from the start of Forest Road 3848, the road forks into two equally-travelled roads. Follow the right fork, uphill. About one-quarter of a mile later, note the big flakes of mica in the roadway and the mica tailing piles on the left. The clearing on the right side of the road is a good place to park.

The Muscovite Mine

The tailing piles are the waste rock and soil from the Muscovite Mine. The rounded tailing piles shine with small pieces of mica, and occasional garnet, beryl or tourmaline crystals. A few small, hardy trees and bushes grow on the piles. The scene is desolate, but beautiful and serene. The view over the valley is extraordinary. Trails through the mine area and the surrounding forest are not wheelchair accessible.

The Muscovite Mine was not named for nearby Moscow, but for the large crystals of muscovite mica found there. Muscovite is a flat transparent rock once valued as insinglass for windows of stoves and carriages. Later, it was used as an insulator in electrical tubes and an additive in paints and lubricants. More than one million dollars in muscovite was removed from this mine.

The Muscovite Mine was one of a half-dozen mines on Mica Mountain at the turn of the century. The claim was first worked in 1888, by two prospectors named Woody and Lamb. For more than eighty years, the Muscovite was closed and reopened under a succession of owners. A large pit was cut into the south face of the mountain and several tunnels followed veins of mica into the rock. When the mica was separated from the surrounding rock, it was removed in pieces of solid muscovite, called books, up to five inches thick and a foot square. The books were hauled down to Deary, then shipped out by rail.

Early in this century, a mining village called Micaville grew around the mine, housing fifteen year-round workers and their families. After World War II, the development of man-made alternatives destroyed the market for muscovite. By 1950, the Muscovite was the only working mine on Mica Mountain, but the operators were searching for beryl, not mica. The blue-green beryl crystals found in the mica deposits had a high beryllium content, and beryllium was a valuable space-age mineral. The Muscovite closed in 1964. Most of the buildings were collapsed by the snow. At the top of the tailings, several hundred yards from the parking area, the face at the end of the pit reveals the intricate swirling layers of white and black rock that forms Mica Mountain.

This is the end of the tour. Retrace your route to Highway 9.

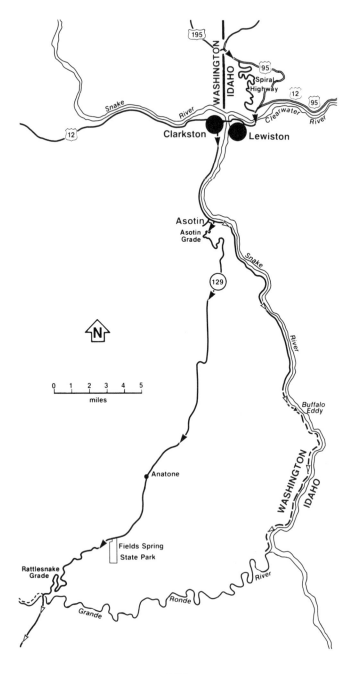

Chapter 12

SPIRALLING DOWN THE HIGHWAYS

(50 miles)

Time: A minimum of one and one-half hour by automobile.

Services: All services are available in Lewiston, Clarkston, and Asotin. Restrooms and drinking water are available at Swallows Park, Chief Looking Glass Park, and at Fields Spring State Park.

Bicycles: This is a good tour for bicyclists who enjoy the challenge of uphill and downhill roads. The Asotin Grade is so steep that some riders dismount and push their bikes. The entire tour follows paved roads, though the roadway shoulders are very narrow on both the Spiral Highway and Rattlesnake Grade portions. The levee parkway trail along the rivers between Lewiston, Clarkston and Asotin is a dream come true for cyclists. The Snake River beaches near Asotin are easily accessible on this bikeway system from either Lewiston or Clarkston. From the end of this tour the nearest towns are Asotin (thirty-four miles retracing the tour) or Enterprise, Oregon (sixty-two miles ahead on Highway 129).

Wheelchairs: This is a good tour for those in wheelchairs, since most of the viewpoints are visible from the roadside. Unless otherwise indicated, all the places described in this chapter are wheelchair accessible.

The highways that spiral down the canyon walls in the southern part of the Inland Empire offer visitors a chance to test their brakes on the way down and their engines on the way up. These roadways provide travelers with remarkable viewpoints to enjoy the beautiful valleys of the Clearwater, Snake, and Grande Ronde Rivers.

This tour begins at the intersection of Highways 95 and 195, eight miles north of Lewiston and ninety miles southeast of Spokane. The roadway descends into the Clearwater River valley and through Lewiston, Idaho, and Clarkston, Washington. It then follows the Snake River upstream to Asotin, winds up the Asotin Grade, then wiggles down Rattlesnake Grade to the Grande Ronde River.

Down The Spiral Highway

At the junction of Highways 95 and 195, go south on Highway 95. One mile ahead, turn right at the crest of the hill, before the Truck Weighing Station. The intersection is marked with a scenic overlook sign. Just past Vista House Gift Shop, stop at the viewpoint on the right.

Below is the confluence of the Clearwater River, which flows from north-central Idaho to the left, and the Snake River which originates near Yellowstone National Park in southern Idaho. The place where the rivers meet is the lowest elevation point in Idaho.

The confluence of the two rivers has a long history as a crossroads and settlement. The Nez Perce regularly met and wintered in the sheltered and warm canyon. They called the place where the waters met Tsceminicum (sigh-MIN-ikum). The Lewis and Clark Expedition camped here on October 10, 1805, on their way to the Pacific. The Columbia and Snake Rivers provided the first highway into the wilderness of Idaho, and beginning in 1861, steamships regularly hauled passengers and freight on the rivers. The village of Lewiston was a thriving community in the 1860s, and the main entry to the gold fields up the Clearwater River (see Chapter 10). In 1863, Lewiston became the first capital of Idaho Territory.

Lewiston has grown to a city of thirty-thousand. The river highway between Lewiston and the Pacific has been tamed by the dams on the Snake and Columbia Rivers. Both cruiseships and barges use the river highway now to carry passengers, grain, and wood products to Portland. Lewiston is the farthest inland seaport on the river system.

The biggest employer in the valley is Potlatch Corporation. From the overlook site, their huge lumber mill and paper manufacturing complex is clearly visible on the eastern edge of Lewiston. The unpleasant odor that occasionally fills the valley is a byproduct of the papermaking process. Visitors sometimes complain about the odor, but local boosters call it the "smell of money." The tan and white circles east of the Potlatch mill are the effluent ponds where paper-manufacturing waste is treated.

Look down from the viewpoint to see the old highway, called the Spiral Highway in honor of its constant curving. When it was built in 1917 it was considered an engineering marvel. In eight miles and thirty curves, the roadway drops more than two-thousand feet, from the edge of the Palouse grainfields at 2,756 feet to the confluence at 738 feet. The Spiral Highway was replaced by a new four-lane highway, so there is virtually no traffic on the old road.

From the viewpoint, visitors can continue on either the new, four-lane Highway 95 or on the old Spiral Highway. The new highway bypasses the romance and a multitude of canyon viewpoints, but it is considerably faster and shorter. The old and new roadways meet at the bottom of the hill at the entrance to Lewiston. To continue the tour on the old road, go downhill straight ahead from the overlook site. The road to the left returns to the new highway.

The canyon wall faces south and bakes to a brown dryness all summer. There is a narrow draw three miles down the Spiral Highway filled with locust trees that survive because of a spring-fed creek there. At one time, a cement tub filled with spring water stood next to the highway on the left. It was a favorite stopping place to refill hot radiators and picnic in the shade. The tub remains, but it is empty now for lack of maintenance.

At the bottom of the hill, the Spiral Highway joins Highways 95 and 12 at the rose garden entrance to Lewiston. The highways meet to cross the Clearwater River on the bridge. Continue south, following the signs for Highway 12 West toward Clarkston. On the right, fifty yards past the rose garden, the Greater Lewiston Chamber of Commerce maintains a small roadside information center, filled with free brochures. The center is staffed by volunteers, and it is usually open from 9 A.M. to 5 P.M. daily. For more information, contact the Chamber of Commerce at 2207 East Main, Lewiston, ID 83501, (208) 743-3531.

The tour continues ahead on Highway 12, crossing the Clearwater River into Lewiston. The highway bypasses Lewiston's downtown by paralleling the levee parkway system. Follow the signs for Highway 12 West to Clarkston.

Up The Snake River

Two miles from the Clearwater River bridge, Highway 12 crosses the Snake River bridge into Washington. After entering Clarkston, note the well-marked junction at the first stoplight fifty yards past the bridge. Turn left onto Highway 129 at this intersection. Highway 129 winds through Clarkston, but is well marked. (For more information about Clarkston, see Chapter 13.)

After leaving Clarkston, Highway 129 parallels the Snake River. On the left is Swallows Park, named for Swallow's Nest, the huge basalt rock on the right ahead. The park is a day-use area with a swimming beach, boat ramp, and grassy picnic areas. Continue past Swallows Park toward Asotin.

Asotin

The town of Asotin is four miles past Swallows Park. It is noted for the rows of lovely old homes built along the roads paralleling the Snake River. Continue on Highway 129, First Street. On the left in the middle of Asotin, the US Corps of Engineers maintains Chief Looking Glass Park, named for one of the great Nez Perce chiefs. This is a beautiful day-use park, has a children's play area, picnic area, and boat launch. Continue ahead on Highway 129 through Asotin.

At the southern edge of Asotin, the highway turns away from the river. At the intersection of First and Washington Streets, turn right, uphill, and follow the signs to Highway 129 South, toward Enterprise.

To The Top Of The Asotin Grade

From the intersection of First and Washington in Asotin, follow Highway 129 up the Asotin Grade toward Anatone. The highway winds through a residential area then passes a sign on the right warning that the next supply of gasoline is seventy-seven miles ahead. The highway through the Grande Ronde River canyon is beautiful, but be prepared, since few supplies or services are available.

The twenty miles between Asotin and the tiny settlement of Anatone are filled with widely scattered grain and cattle ranches on a windy and slightly rolling plateau. The views of the surrounding mountains and canyons are delightful. Anatone has a post office and cafe and a few homes, but no other services. Past the town, the trees begin crowding toward the highway and the fields are smaller. For three miles past Anatone, the highway climbs to Rattlesnake Summit, at 3,965 feet elevation. One mile later, turn left into Fields Spring State Park.

Fields Spring State Park

The half-mile-long driveway to the park winds through a lovely old-growth forest of fir and pine. The big trees are surprising after a long drive through the dry open country from Asotin to Anatone. Another surprise is the ecological diversity contained within the 445-acre park. One hundred and fifty-one plant species have been documented within the park, ranging from wetland species like ferns to desert plants like sagebrush. The trails in the park cross a multitude of ecological zones. Those zones have varying plants, birds, and animals. The diversity of the park is remarkable, but perhaps the best thing about Fields Spring is its quiet and beauty. The park is the busiest in the winter when the cross-country skiers arrive. During the warm-weather months it is virtually empty.

The park is open daily, and rangers provide interpretive programs and nature walks upon request. Modern restrooms, picnic shelters, a children's playground, and hot showers are available. Contact the park at PO Box 37, Anatone, WA 99401, (509) 256-3332.

The Old Man of the River

Twenty-five years ago, a cruise into Hells Canyon was often a one-way trip. The foaming rapids and jagged rocks of North America's deepest gorge regularly shattered the boats and boatmen who tested its waters.

The jet-powered boat with the welded aluminum hull was the solution. The propellerless jet pump came from New Zealand. The jet was mounted in a hull tough enough to stand the pounding and twisting of the Canyon. Welded aluminum boats have no rivets or screws to loosen and no fiberglass or wood to shatter. With about half the weight of conventional boats and an extremely shallow draft, they travel through water six inches (or less) in depth. Norm Riddle created the first welded aluminum jet boats at his shop in Lewiston.

"He built four twenty-four-foot boats in the fall of 1964, the first ever, two for local outfitters and two for loggers to use on their river log drives. They were ugly boats, Riddle said, but they worked — they would take you upriver and bring you back."

Edie & Norm Riddle; a jet-pump nozzle is visible on the left.

Jet boats created several new industries for Lewiston. More than a dozen local companies now build jet boats. Thirty million dollars worth of jet boats, most manufactured in the Lewiston area, are sold annually. One local manufacturer is Weldcraft, the company started by Norm Riddle in 1968, and now owned by his son Doug. Doug offers free guided tours of his factory, on weekdays from 8 A.M. to 5 P.M. Weldcraft is at 607 Snake River Avenue, Lewiston, ID 83501, (208) 746-3976.

The second jet boat industry is river touring. Two dozen guides, based in Lewiston, Clarkston and Asotin, offer fishing, hunting or river-watching trips up the Snake and Salmon Rivers. One of the jet boat guides is Norm Riddle. In 1978, at fifty years of age, he retired from boat-building to operate Snake River Outfitters of Lewiston. He comments:

> I came to this area in 1950, and put my boats
> in the water as soon as I arrived. When I dis-
> covered the rivers of this valley, I had to be on
> them. I was going upriver every weekend, taking
> friends, and then I decided to make it a business,
> so I became a river guide. In 1970, I bought
> property in Hells Canyon.

He built the Kirby Creek Lodge, which is the destination for his guided trips. It is the only private land remaining in the heart of Hells Canyon.

Now, Riddle's life is the river. His craggy face reflects the hours in the sun and spray of the canyons. He stays, as much as possible, at the lodge. His wife, Edie, is the company cook and deckhand.

Norm Riddle built the first welded aluminum jet boat, he has run the river as many times as anyone, and he owns the only lodge inside the upper canyon. Those accomplishments justify his local nickname, the "Old Man of the River."

An Oasis on the River

William Renfrew, an attorney and big game hunter, retired in the Grand Ronde River canyon. His daughter, Farrel Vail says: "My father hunted and fished all over the world, but he picked this spot because he could shoot or catch something right out his door every day of the year."

The abundance of wildlife that inspired Renfrew to buy the Rocking R Ranch remains today. The steelhead and salmon still migrate on the Grande Ronde, the deer and elk still graze the hillsides, the bear and cougar still prowl the canyons, the grouse and pheasants fly through the meadows, and the wild sheep and goats still patrol the mountaintops.

Bill and Farrel Vail bought the Rocking R in 1975, two years after her father died. Ten years later, in a "weak moment," they bought Boggan's Oasis, a nearby restaurant. Farrel now lives here year round, while Bill is closing their office-supply store in Alaska. The Vails operate the only traveler's services along the lower Grande Ronde. Boggan's Oasis is a full-service restaurant and the home of the famous old-fashioned milk shake — twenty ounces of hard ice cream, drowned in fruit syrup, and served in a glass with the tin blender cup on the side. The Rocking R is a local bed and breakfast lodge, as well as the Vail's home. The Oasis and the Rocking R form a "mini-resort," a friendly destination in some of the wildest country in the Inland Empire. For Farrel, who looks ten years younger than her fifty-plus years, it's just what she wanted.

"I planned to retire here, but I saw the potential for a business," she explained. "I spent twenty-five years in festival management and then in retail business and I got tired of the rat race. I don't care now if I ever go to town. I spent years travelling and I like the quiet — plus, the people here are absolutely wonderful. Here, the wildlife is beautiful and I don't ever have to fight traffic. It's home."

To resume the tour, return to Highway 129 and turn left, downhill, toward Enterprise, Oregon.

Rattlesnake Grade

The ten-mile descent from Rattlesnake Summit to the banks of the Grande Ronde River is another Spiral Highway known as Rattlesnake Grade. The road is narrow and very winding with 110 curves in ten miles. Beautiful views of the canyon walls and the river valley open at every turn. During May and June, the hills are filled with wildflowers. Cattle share the hillsides with deer, mountain sheep, bear and elk. The canyon has few human residents because it is too rocky, steep and desolate. Its beauty is in the stark and rugged scenery. Continue ahead until Highway 129 crosses the river.

Adjacent to the Boggan's Oasis restaurant, south of the Highway 129 bridge, the Washington Fish and Game Department maintains a free river-access area for rafters and anglers. Camping and picnicking are allowed there. Pit toilets and a primitive launch ramp are provided, but drinking water is not available. Three similar river-access areas are located within five miles of the highway bridge.

The Grande Ronde River carved this canyon. Like the Snake and Clearwater, the Grande Ronde sliced downward through layers of basalt rock, creating a beautiful gorge of stair-stepping black cliffs. The Grande Ronde is virtually unroaded from the Highway 129 bridge downstream to the confluence with the Snake River. This canyon's beauty and isolation make it a favorite for visitors in rafts and canoes.

This tour ends when Highway 129 crosses the river. The Oregon border is four miles ahead on Highway 129. The first town ahead on Highway 129 is Enterprise, Oregon, sixty-two miles south. Asotin is thirty-four miles back along the tour route. Just before the bridge, County Road 100, a gravelled road paralleling the river upstream, winds sixteen miles to the tiny town of Troy, Oregon.

This tour ends at the bottom of the grade. All directions from this point are uphill, through one of the most beautiful and unpopulated portions of the Inland Empire.

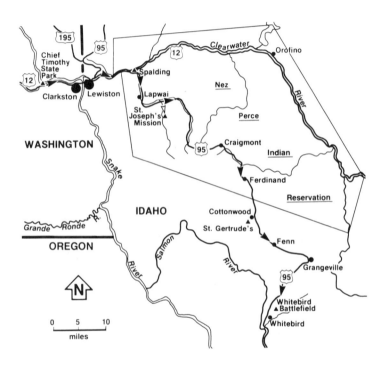

Chapter 13

IN THE LAND OF THE NEZ PERCE

(107 miles)

Time: A minimum of two hours by automobile.

Services: Services are available at regular intervals in towns and parks along the route.

Bicycles: The entire tour is paved, and many sections are well suited for bicycles. The road from Chief Timothy Park through Lapwai follows the rivers and is flat, beautiful, and has wide shoulders. Another perfect bicycling route follows the levee system around Lewiston and Clarkston. For twenty-six miles, a wide paved biking and walking pathway connects both towns and both rivers.

From Lapwai to the Camas Prairie near Cottonwood, the highway is narrow, often steep, and must be shared with many trucks. This is a dangerous section for bicyclists. On the Camas Prairie, from Cottonwood through Grangeville and down to White Bird, the roadway is usually wide enough for safe bicycling, but traffic remains heavy. The highway is mostly flat to Grangeville, then steepens.

Wheelchairs: Unless otherwise indicated, all of the places described in this chapter are wheelchair accessible.

The Nez Perce were one of the most powerful tribes in the Inland Empire. Before the white settlers arrived, Nez Perce bands controlled 13,700,000 acres in northeastern Oregon, southeastern Washington and north-central Idaho. They wintered in the warm canyons, and spent the summers in the highlands hunting and gathering. Their prowess on horseback and their knowledgeable breeding of Appaloosa horses enhanced their reputation as skilled warriors.

The Nez Perce (meaning "pierced nose" in French, was applied by French trappers) were respected as honorable and friendly. Those gentle traits were first noted by the explorers Lewis and Clark. The exploration party was near death from starvation when they stumbled upon a Nez Perce camp in 1805. The Nez Perce saved their lives.

This tour visits the heart of Nez Perce country, beginning at Alpowai Creek where Chiefs Timothy and Red Wolf lived, then following Highways 12 and 95 south along the Clearwater River then across the Camas Prairie. The tour ends at White Bird, where the Nez Perce defeated a larger force of US Army regulars in 1877.

Chief Timothy State Park

This tour begins at Chief Timothy State Park in southeastern Washington state. The park is on Highway 12, about ninety miles east of Walla Walla, and eight miles west of Clarkston, at the confluence of the Snake River and Alpowai Creek.

The first stop is the Alpowai Interpretive Center at the park entrance. The center's exhibits trace the development of the area from settlement by the Nez Perce, the visit by Lewis and Clark, later white settlement, and the damming of the Snake River. A twenty-minute slide show is free. The center is open afternoons only, Wednesday through Sunday, during the summer.

Most of Chief Timothy State Park is an island connected to the Interpretive Center by a short auto bridge. The park includes a day-use area that includes a sandy beach, picnic shelters, a boat launch ramp, a children's play area, and a concession stand. The campground offers thirty-three hookup sites at $9.50 per night and seventeen no-hookup sites at seven dollars per night. Most of the island is reserved as a wildlife refuge area open to hiking. Docks and moorage areas are scattered among the campgounds. Chief Timothy Park is often full on summer weekends. For more information, contact Chief Timothy State Park, Highway 12, Clarkston, WA 99403, (509) 758-9580.

The tour leaves the park on Highway 12 headed east. Several day-use areas are available along the highway for picnicking and birdwatching. These day-use areas offer access to the wildlife refuges along the river.

After leaving the park, note the black rocks that form the steep canyon walls along the river. This basalt rock was deposited by eruptions during the Miocene Era, six to seventeen million years ago. During an eleven-million-year period, liquid rock flowed outward from cracks or fissures in the surface and gradually filled most of the Columbia River Basin. Geologists suspect that 120 to 150 separate eruptions occurred. Each eruption produced a new layer, some layers are up to four-hundred feet thick, with an average thickness of about fifty to one hundred feet. The Snake and Clearwater Rivers gradually wore away the rock, creating the deep valleys and revealing those layers.

Three miles from the park entrance, on the hillside to the right, note the variety of forms the basalt has assumed: regular six-sided columns, pillow shapes, and solid blocks. A mile later, on the right, notice a well-defined layer of regular basalt columns.

Across the Snake River to the north (left) at mile 4 is the Port of Wilma. Wilma is one of two dozen ports along the waterway system created by the eight dams on the Columbia/Snake river highway. Barges regularly transport grain and wood products to Portland, where they are transferred to ocean-going freighters. (More information about the dams and locks appears in Chapter 2.) This section of the tour provides a great vantage point to watch barges being loaded at the port. Continue ahead toward Clarkston.

Clarkston

Six miles from the park entrance, note the historical marker on the right. It explains the passage of Lewis and Clark on this section of river. The west-bound exploration party camped on the north side of the river on October 10, 1805. The explorers' names were later given to the two cities, Lewiston on the Idaho side of the river, and Clarkston on the Washington side.

In Clarkston, Highway 12 becomes Bridge Street. At the first stoplight in the town, at Fifth Street, Clarkston's new convention and recreation center is on the left, and the Clarkston Chamber of Commerce is on the right.

Around Lewiston

The tour continues on Bridge Street (Highway 12) headed east toward Lewiston. When crossing the Snake River bridge, stay in the right lane and follow the Highway 12 to the East as the road circles under the bridge and around Lewiston. The highway follows the levees built along the city's river shoreline. Adjacent to this section of highway are several access points to the levee walkway system. Picnic tables, ponds with ducks and geese, shaded grassy areas, a twenty-six- mile-long walkway/bikeway system, drinking water and restrooms are available along the levees. (Additional information about Lewiston appears in Chapter 12.)

Up The Clearwater

Two and one-half miles from the bridge over the Snake, Highway 12 crosses the Clearwater River which separates Lewiston from North Lewiston. About one-half mile after crossing the Clearwater River Bridge, Highway 12 joins Highway 95. Follow the combined Highway 12 East and Highway 95 South along the Clearwater River. This section of river is free-flowing, wide, and beautiful. The river is named Clearwater for a good reason. After leaving the Lewiston area, the canyon narrows, and except for a few ranches and scattered businesses, the riverbanks are unpopulated.

One-half mile from the junction of the two highways, at 31st Street, is the first of many access points for anglers, boaters and picnickers. This section of river is maintained as wildlife habitat for ducks and geese. Grain has been planted as forage for waterfowl, and nesting boxes have been built. The access points are well-marked.

The levee walkway/bikeway system continues on the north shore
of the Clearwater adjacent to the highway. The pathway ends at Hatwai
Creek, which is the eastern edge of the Nez Perce Reservation. The
reservation includes 88,000 acres along the Clearwater River and
across the Camas Prairie. This tour continues through the reservation
until it crosses the southern boundary near Cottonwood.

Two historic markers are at the pullout on the right, six miles
from the Clearwater River Bridge. One marker indicates that this was
the site of a Nez Perce encampment for about ten-thousand years. The
other marker explains the Nez Perce legend about Coyote's Fishnet,
which explains a rocky area nearby.

Highways 12 and 95 separate eight miles from the Clearwater
Bridge. This tour follows Highway 95. Two miles past the highway
intersection, on the left, is the headquarters of the Nez Perce National
Historic Park at Spalding. This is an important stop for those who wish
to understand both Nez Perce culture and the sites ahead.

Spalding

In 1836, Reverend Henry Harmon Spalding and his wife Eliza
came to Idaho, the first American family to settle this wilderness. The
Spaldings crossed the continent with the Whitmans, whose lives are
detailed in Chapter 3.

The Spaldings were missionaries who brought Christianity and
agriculture to the Nez Perce. By 1841, the Spaldings' grist mill was
producing flour and their sawmill was cutting lumber. When the
Whitmans were killed in 1847, the Spaldings left Idaho and moved to
Oregon. (They returned to the area after the Indian Wars.) Their
mission disappeared; later the Nez Perce office of the Bureau of Indian
Affairs occupied the location. The Spalding site is now the headquarters for the Nez Perce National Historic Park. The park is a
collection of twenty-four historic sites scattered throughout the Nez
Perce Reservation. The Visitor Center at Spalding is the place to begin
an investigation of the park.

At the Visitor Center, tribal culture is explained with a series of
displays of Nez Perce village life, ancient food-gathering tools and

The Best Cowboy Was An Indian

The Nez Perce maintain a well-earned reputation for their riding skill. They developed the Appaloosa breed, and were well-respected by their foes, including the US Army, for their horsemanship. A Nez Perce named Jackson Sundown won the World Saddle Bronc Riding Championship in 1916, the only full-blooded Indian to hold a rodeo championship title.

The place was the Pendleton Round-Up, when Sundown was fifty years old, competing in a young man's sport against cowboys half his age. He competed in earlier rodeos for the world title, but the award always went to others, despite what many recognized were Sundown's superior rides. Some thought the judges were unwilling to bestow the title on an Indian.

Sundown vowed that the 1916 competition would be his last. His seemingly-reckless bronc-riding style and incredible native abilities earned him the respect of his competitors and the favor of the rodeo spectators. Sundown outlasted the other cowboys, and successfully rode a jack-knifing bronco named Angel, but the judges insisted that he ride twice more. The accusations again surfaced that his rightful prize was again refused because of his Nez Perce ancestry.

Finally, the judges could no longer dispute his masterful riding abilities. Jackson Sundown was awarded the title of World Champion and a share of the $6,500 in prize money. Later, he was elected to the Pendleton Round-Up Hall of Fame. Waible Patton, a pioneer Pendleton photographer, was at the 1916 Round-Up. His report of the bronc-riding competition appears in Bill Gulick's book, *Chief Joseph Country:*

> Yes, the story about Jackson Sundown is a true one. Father took me when I was just a kid, and I was there. They made Sundown do several re-rides.... It was getting late in the day, and the

sun was going down in the west. It seemed like everybody in the crowd was yelling: 'Sundown! Sundown! Sundown!' When he finished the ride, the judges gave him the title. Whether there would have been trouble if they hadn't, I don't know, but Jackson was a good rider and he really deserved to win. I witnessed the event and it is a true story.

Jackson Sundown was born in 1866. His father was Cool-cool-thla and his mother was Cap-te-a-ti-moi. Chief Joseph was his uncle. As a lad of ten and eleven, he fought in the Nez Perce War of 1877, where he was wounded three times. After Chief Joseph surrendered, Sundown became a renegade, living among the Flatheads in Montana. When he made clandestine visits to the Nez Perce Reservation, he faced imprisonment if captured. On several occasions he was chased back into Montana by the US Army. Because of his illegal status, he could not claim his rightful allotment of tribal land in Idaho.

The Flatheads were generous with the Nez Perce renegades who lived among them. Sundown was given an allotment of land on the Flathead Reservation. He married Pewlosap, a Flathead, in 1894. She took the name Annie Jackson Sundown. They had three daughters, one who died in infancy, Rosalia, who died at age 13, and Adeline Redsky, who lived to be almost one-hundred years old. Sundown divorced Annie in 1909 and returned to his homeland. In 1913, he married a Nez Perce, Cecilia Pe-lot-son-my, and they lived along Mission Creek between Lapwai and Culdesac. Bureau of Indian Affairs records indicate they had no children.

When Sundown died on December 18, 1923, his total estate was a fifty dollar per month payment he received from the federal government. A hearing officer gave half the estate to his widow and half to his daughter, Adeline Redsky Sundown Woodcock.

Jackson Sundown is buried at St. Joseph's Mission. To locate the cemetery, turn off Highway 95 at the Jacques Spur road, following the signs toward St. Joseph's Mission. Four miles from Highway 95, turn left onto the last driveway before the church, and park near the fence, fifty feet straight ahead. Go through the wire fence and continue 100 feet up the hill to the cemetery. The cemetery gate is on the far corner. Many graves are overgrown and unkempt, but Sundown's grave is well-tended. Many remember the greatest of the Nez Perce cowboys.

methods, and crafts. Some contemporary tribal crafts are available for sale. A free slide show about Nez Perce history is shown on request. A free map of the entire park, showing the location of all twenty-four sites, is available, and knowledgeable staff are on duty to answer questions about the tribe or the park. A brochure and map about the White Bird battlefield at the end of this tour is available for fifty cents. The Visitor Center is open daily. For more information, contact the park at PO Box 93, Spalding, ID 83551, (208) 843-2261.

The site of the Spalding Mission is one-quarter mile east of the Visitor Center. A beautiful riverside picnic area, complete with restrooms and drinking water, surrounds the mission site. Several old buildings dating from the Nez Perce Indian Agency period still remain. Plenty of National Park Service historical markers are scattered around the picnic area. The old cemetery, where the Spaldings were buried, adjoins the picnic area.

Toward The Camas Prairie

The tour follows Highway 95 south from Spalding, leaving the Clearwater River canyon and continuing up Lapwai Creek. Three miles past Spalding, the highway passes the town of Lapwai and the headquarters of the Nez Perce tribe.

Seven miles past Lapwai is Jacques Spur, at the junction of Mission Creek Road and Highway 95. A cafe marks the intersection. St. Joseph's Mission Church and the cemetery, where Jackson Sundown is buried, are four miles down Mission Creek Road, to the right.

Highway 95 beyond Jacques Spur is narrow and winding as it follows the steep canyons. The Camas Prairie Railroad roughly parallels the highway. The first of many wonderful old railway trestles can be seen on the left about eight miles past Jacques Spur.

As the highway reaches the top of the long grade up from the river, about fourteen miles from Jacques Spur, Highway 95 enters a very productive agricultural area known as Camas Prairie. The gently rolling land is planted mostly to wheat. The name refers to the bulbs dug in the meadows by the Nez Perce. The small bulbs were the most important carbohydrate source in the tribal diet. The camas is a member of the lily family and produces a showy blue flowerstalk in May and June. Early settlers often remarked about the beauty of the camas fields, looking so much like blue lakes. The tour remains on the Camas Prairie until the road steepens again past Grangeville.

Seven miles across the prairie is Craigmont, a town with an unusual history. In 1908 two towns, Vollmer and Ilo, were built on opposite sides of the railroad tracks here. For twelve years, the two villages competed with two sets of banks, retail stores and schools. The rivalry ended when they merged in 1920 to form the town of Craigmont. The town park is on the right side of the highway, at the south end of town, just before the railroad bridge. The park offers shaded picnic tables, drinking water, and restrooms.

Highway 95 will soon bypass Craigmont. The new highway also will bypass Lawyer's Canyon, a beautiful, winding and tree-shaded portion of Highway 95 south of Craigmont.

Nine miles from Craigmont, the highway bisects the village of Ferdinand. About five miles past Ferdinand, the tour leaves the Nez Perce Reservation.

Cottonwood

Ten miles past Ferdinand, turn right onto Business Highway 95. Cottonwood, population one-thousand, is one-half mile down this road. Part of the downtown section features a sidewalk roof, giving the town an air of Western charm. A small community park, complete with drinking water, restrooms, picnic tables and a children's play area, is at the corner of King and Butler Streets, on the north side of town.

Cottonwood's claim to fame is the Priory of St. Gertrude's. The Benedictine nuns established their convent and school here in 1907. The beautiful chapel and priory building was built of local rock and finished in 1924. Two years later, the nuns opened a school. The school experienced financial problems in the 1960s and the building was converted to a public high school. Approximately 110 Benedictine sisters call St. Gertrude's their home, though many work at schools and hospitals throughout the state.

To find the priory, follow King Street (Business Highway 95) for one mile until it ends at Front Street. Turn right, and continue on Front Street for two miles. The priory is the huge building on the knoll overlooking the prairie. The building was recently listed in the National Historical Register. The lovely chapel, which is not wheelchair accessible, is open daily. The ornate altar came from Germany.

Adjacent to the priory is St. Gertrude's Museum, one of the best in the Inland Empire. The collection was started by Sister Alfreda Elsensohn. It includes biological specimens, mineral samples, Vietnamese cultural objects, and artifacts left by Polly Bemis and Buckskin Bill. Polly Bemis came to the Salmon River country as a Chinese slave. Buckskin Bill was a modern mountain man who made his own tools and guns. The museum also houses an amazing collection of old household utensils, including the baby bottle for twins and horse snowshoes. In 1988, Samuel Emmanuel donated his wife Winifred's, collection of rare Oriental and European antique furniture and ceramics to the museum. This collection contains dozens of unique and exquisite pieces; it's a wondrous sight in this out-of-the-way location.

The museum is usually open during daylight hours. Visitors can phone ahead to insure that the museum will be open, or they can ask one of the nuns to open the museum. For museum guides, there are no better than the sisters of St. Gertrude's. The museum is free, though donations are accepted. The mailing address is St. Gertrude's Priory, Cottonwood, ID 83522, (208) 962-3224 or 962-7123.

To continue the tour, return to Highway 95 and turn right (south). The mountains that form the southern and eastern boundaries of the Camas Prairie are visible now. The pullout by the historic markers, on the left side of the highway, two miles past Cottonwood junction, is a great place to survey the prairie landscape. Picnic tables are available but no drinking water or restrooms are provided. The markers commemorate the battles of July, 1877, between the Nez Perce and local settlers. Continue on Highway 95 South toward Grangeville.

Grangeville

Grangeville, the biggest urban center on the prairie, with a population of about 3,500, is on Highway 95 about fifteen miles from

A Taste of the Old West

The oldest complete custom saddle-making company in the US is in downtown Grangeville. A tour of the Ray Holes Saddle Company offers visitors a chance to enjoy unsurpassed craftsmanship and Western friendliness.

"Coming here is as close to a taste of the Old West as you can get today," said Gerald Ray Holes, owner and son of the company founder, Ray Holes. "Lots of our tools are more than one hundred years old; we make saddles the way they should be made, they way they were made."

Ray Holes saddles are made with no shortcuts, and no sacrifices of quality. Saddle-making begins with a wooden framework, or "tree", built to the specifications of the horse and rider. Layers of rawhide and leather are then fitted onto that frame. The fancy leather tooling that creates attractive floral patterns on the finished saddle is then added by hand, without the use of any patterns or preprinted designs. The result is a unique and beautiful work of art that is also fully functional and fitted to the exact needs of the buyer.

This is really the Cadillac end of the industry, we just want our customers to feel that they got the best. We have all we can do to fill our orders — we always have about a year's worth of work waiting for us — and we do what we want, concentrating on quality, not quantity.

They make about fifty riding saddles every year, plus approximately 150 pack saddles and plenty of bridles, halters and other tack. The riding saddles begin at $1,650, and average about $2,000 each. The most expensive saddle they've created was their unique Fiftieth Anniversary Saddle, valued at approximately $15,000 and now in a private collection in Maryland. Most of their sales are by mail order, to riders in North America, Europe, and Asia.

Gerald Ray Holes

This top-of-the-line saddlery began in 1934, when Ray Holes opened a leather repair shop at his ranch near Cottonwood. Two years later, he opened Ray Holes Saddle Company, in Cottonwood. Three years later, it moved to Grangeville. It has never deviated from Ray Holes' committment to quality.

Ray's son, Gerald Ray, grew up around the store, and learned the craft from his father. Gerald went to college, graduated, and worked for a half-dozen years as an industrial arts teacher before returning to the family business in 1969. He and his wife, Ellamae, bought the business from his parents. Now he works in the shop doing the fancy leather tooling and she is the office manager and part-time tour guide.

"We get people all the time; we like to have them," Gerald said. Visitors are given free guided tours of both the retail sales area (the company sells Western boots and clothing, as well as their own riding gear) and the leather shop. Then the visitors are free to wander about the shop or store and ask questions of the craftsmen at work. The atmosphere is relaxed and friendly—in the tradition of genuine Western hospitality.

The Ray Holes Saddle Company is at 213 West Main Street in downtown Grangeville, Idaho 83530; phone (208) 983-1460. The store is open from 8:30 A.M. to 5:30 P.M. weekdays and from 9 A.M. to 5 P.M. on Saturday. No appointments are required. Dozens of beautiful pieces of Western art and artifacts line the walls. For anyone who appreciates hand-crafted beauty, or who wants a glimpse into the life of the Old West, a tour of Ray Holes Saddle Company is a must.

Cottonwood junction. To visit Grangeville, turn left onto Highway 13, which is the town's main street.

The US Forest Service's Forest Supervisors Office at the eastern edge of Grangeville provides information on nearby rafting, camping, hunting or fishing. The White Bird Battlefield Auto Tour brochure, which is very useful to have along during the last part of this tour, is available there for fifty cents. Contact the Nez Perce Forest Supervisors Office at Rt. 2, Box 475, Grangeville, ID 83530, (208) 983-1950.

To continue the tour, follow Highway 95 South. Six miles past Grangeville, the historical marker on the right side of the highway offers a great view of the Camas Prairie. During the 1877 war, the Nez Perce camped at the small lake below the viewpoint. Past the pulloff, the highway rises steeply for two miles to the top of the White Bird Hill.

White Bird

From the summit of White Bird Hill, Highway 95 continues downhill at a seven percent grade for eight miles until it reaches the Salmon River. This rugged mountain range was impassable until the first winding road was constructed in 1921. A large pullout on the left side of the highway, about three-quarters of a mile from the summit, provides a wonderful view of the Salmon River canyon. The old highway is visible on the hillsides below. Picnic tables are provided at this pullout, but drinking water and restrooms are not available.

At Milepost 230, about a mile from the summit, turn left onto the old highway. This tour follows the old highway to the bottom of the grade at the town of White Bird. The old highway is four miles longer than the new highway, but it offers a leisurely descent, roadside vistas, and a close-up view of battle sites of the 1877 Nez Perce War.

The tour continues down the old highway. Turn left onto the paved road opposite Milepost 230. Red marker posts have been placed along the road. The posts correspond to stops numbered on the self-guided tour brochure entitled "White Bird Battlefield Auto Tour," which was available at Spalding and at the Forest Service Supervisor's office in Grangeville.

The first red post is at a pullout on the left side of the road, a mile from Highway 95. From this spot, visitors can see the route the US Army took toward the Nez Perce encampment at White Bird. Approximately one-hundred soldiers under Capt. David Perry rode down the hill from Grangeville early in the morning of July 17, 1877, expecting to attack the Nez Perce camp at the bottom of the hill. Their line of march is visible from this stop.

The second post is on the left side of the road, six miles from Highway 95. From a viewpoint this pullout, visitors can see where the army advance guard was positioned when the soldiers noticed the Nez Perce below. The trumpeter started to blow the battle call, but was killed by a long-distance bullet from a Nez Perce marksman. Just below the pullout is a grave on the right side of the road, marking the burial place of an army sergeant.

The third post is located on the left side of the road, seven miles from the highway. To the southwest of this viewpoint, the army forces were quickly outflanked by the Nez Perce. The Army had more men and better guns, but the Nez Perce had superior tactics and horses. Though they were outnumbered, the Nez Perce quickly surrounded and attacked the cavalry, forcing an unceremonious retreat back up the hill. The Nez Perce killed thirty-four soldiers, and lost none of their own. The Nez Perce then retreated as larger army forces began searching for them. Being outnumbered and out gunned, Chief Joseph began his Long March which ended when he surrendered to the U.S. Army in the Bear Paw Mountains of Montana.

The town of White Bird is two miles past the third post, where the old and new Highway 95 rejoin. The tour ends here.

A Cool Treat at the Cougar Creamery!

Pullman visitors who like cold ice cream on hot days will find the best at Ferdinand's. Ferdinand's is a retail ice cream shop maintained by the Washington State University Creamery.

WSU is a land-grant university with a strong animal-science program. One of the products of raising cows and dairy research is milk. WSU uses milk from university cows to produce their old-fashioned, all-natural, finest-quality ice cream and cheese.

Students, alumni, professors and visitors all meet at Ferdinand's to buy fifteen flavors of ice cream and eighteen flavors of milk shakes. Sundaes, sodas, and banana splits also are available. Ferdinand's sells about three hundred gallons of ice cream every month.

Ferdinand's also is the place to select from their eight flavors of cheese. The local favorite is "Cougar Gold," named for the WSU mascot. Cougar Gold is made like a cheddar, but with the addition of additional cultures, which strengthen the flavor. The cheeses are sold in thirty-ounce tins. About 100,000 tins are produced annually.

The Creamery is a learning laboratory for animal-science and food-science classes. WSU students also work in the dairy, creamery, and retail store to get hands-on experience in all aspects of the business.

Ferdinand's is in Troy Hall, about one block south of the Compton Union Building at the center of campus. It is open weekdays from 9 A.M. to 4 P.M. Contact Ferdinand's, WSU, Pullman, WA 99164, (509) 335-4014.

Index

About the Author

Bill London lives in Moscow, Idaho. He and his family moved to the Inland Empire in 1975 and purchased twenty acres of timberland near St. Maries, Idaho. In one year, he and his partner, Gina Gormley, built an octagonal log cabin, which was their home for nine years. Their daughter, Willow, was born in 1978.

Tired of working at odd jobs, he sought employment that was both at-home and creative — and tried writing. Relying on luck, and the experience generated by a basketfull of rejection notices, he sold his first article in 1981. It was so much fun that he never stopped.

Now, he has had five hundred articles published in newspapers and magazines nationwide. Most focus on travel or outdoor topics. He is a member of the American Society of Journalists and Authors, and the Northwest Outdoor Writers Association. This is his first book.